The Multinational Corporation and the Resource Cost of International Technology Transfer

The Multinational Corporation and the Resource Cost of International Technology Transfer

David J. Teece

Ballinger Publishing Company • Cambridge, Massachusetts
A Subsidiary of J.B. Lippincott Company

T
174.3
T43
1976

 This book is printed on recycled paper.

International Standard Book Number: 0-88410-053-7

Library of Congress Catalog Card Number: 76-26053

Printed in the United States of America

3 3001 00594 3773

Library of Congress Cataloging in Publication Data

Teece, David J.
 The multinational corporation and the resource cost of international technology transfer.

 Includes bibliographical references.
 1. Technology transfer. 2. International business enterprises. I. Title.
T174.3.T43   1977   338.4'5   76-26053
ISBN 0-88410-053-7

To my mother and father.

Contents

List of Figures

List of Tables

Acknowledgments

I would like to acknowledge the financial support provided for this study by the National Science Foundation, under a grant to Professor Edwin Mansfield of the University of Pennsylvania. Gratitude is also expressed to the Penfield Fellowship fund of the University of Pennsylvania which was a source of additional support in the preliminary stages of the research. The trenchant comments of Professor Mansfield were much appreciated during all phases of the study. Professors Irving Kravis and Herbert Levine made useful observations on the final draft. My particular gratitude goes the participating firms, without whose cooperation this study would not have been possible.

The Multinational Corporation and the Resource Cost of International Technology Transfer

 *Chapter One*

Introduction

I.1 TECHNOLOGY TRANSFER AND THE INTERNATIONAL ECONOMY

Imported technology in one form or another has a pervasive influence on the daily lives of most of the world's population. Historically, technology has moved from one part of the world to another by a creeping process of diffusion. More recently, technology is being transferred purposefully and more rapidly. However, the resultant diffusion has been quite uneven in its geographical impact, and there is concern that the "technology gap"[1] between the developed countries and the less-developed countries is widening.

Concern about the widening of the gap and the need for international technology transfer seems to be rooted in the comparatively recent acceptance of the notion that the application of modern technology is the very essence of economic growth and development. Simon Kuznets has argued:

Whatever the source, the increase in the stock of useful knowledge and the extension of its application are of the essence of modern economic growth. . . . No matter where these technological and social innovations emerge—and they are largely the products of the developed countries—the economic growth of any given nation depends upon their adoption. In that sense, whatever the national affiliation of resources used, any single nation's economic growth has its base somewhere outside its boundaries— with the single exception of the pioneering nation. . . . Indeed this dependence of a single nation's growth on the transnational stock of useful knowledge is implicit in the concept of an economic epoch.[2]

According to this view, economic growth in all but the pioneering nation is heavily dependent on foreign technological and social innovation and their international diffusion.

I.2 IMPORTANCE OF THE COST OF INTERNATIONAL TECHNOLOGY TRANSFER

Since modern economic growth depends on the successful application of modern technology, it is important to understand the factors that influence the worldwide application of new technology. Very little attention seems to have been given this issue in the literature. Accordingly, it seems necessary to move toward identifying sets of factors that are likely to influence the international transfer and application of technology. It is plausible that a dominant consideration in the international transfer of technology is the cost of transfer. Kenneth Arrow, for instance, has stated that:

> The understanding of transmission of knowledge is of special importance in two of the key socioeconomic problems of our time: (a) international inequalities in productivity, and (b) the failure of the educational system in reducing income inequality. The two problems have a considerable formal similarity. If one nation or class has the knowledge which enables it to achieve high productivity, why is not the other acquiring that information? That a nation or class has a consistently high productivity implies a successful communication system within the nation or class, so the problem turns on the differential between costs of communication within and between classes.[3]

The suggestion seems to be that transfer costs represent a measure of the resources used in transferring an innovation and are at least to some degree an indicator of the ease or difficulty of technology transfer.

While the above quotation reflects a macro concern with the problems and costs of transmitting and absorbing information, these issues are also important at the micro level. In particular, they confront firms involved in technology transfer, irrespective of whether the transfer occurs domestically from one manufacturing facility to another, or internationally from a manufacturing facility in one country to another abroad. The successful transfer of a technical innovation requires the transmission and absorption of a great deal of information, technical and organizational. It is often felt that an important attribute of the multinational firm is its ability to perform this function efficiently. However, very little is known about how the task of transfer is performed, the resources employed or the costs and problems involved. Economists freely admit that at both the analytical and the factual level, very little is known about the international transmission of know-how.[4]

I.3 TECHNOLOGY TRANSFER COSTS: LEVEL AND DETERMINANTS

Given the considerable significance that can be attached to the costs of technology transfer, it is of some importance to know the level of these costs and the factors that determine them. An examination of the process of innovation and the market for technology will be the starting point for a discussion of this matter.

It is widely recognized that the notion of technical change as a factor that shifts the production function without imposing any substantial demands on resource inputs is an inadequate characterization of the process of technical change. Clearly, models of disembodied technical change err in assuming that technology falls like manna on all firms. However, while it is generally recognized that it takes substantial investment in order to make a product or process feasible, it is common to argue that once this has been accomplished, the costs of transferring the innovation to another firm are very much less. Marginal costs are allegedly unimportant compared to average costs. In other words the first entity can gain knowledge only after great effort, but once this knowledge has been attained, other entities can acquire it with ease once access is granted. Supporters of this view contend that for theoretical purposes it is an appropriate abstraction to assume that the transmission of technology between firms and between countries is costless.[5]

The contention of this study is that the proposition that transfer costs are essentially trivial needs to be tested. While some kinds of knowledge might require trivial transfer costs, the costs of transferring technical knowledge may be nontrivial. Aside from royalty payments, which are in the nature of economic rents, substantial resources might have to be utilized not only to transmit technical information, but also to ensure its successful absorption. "Only the broad outline of technical knowledge is codified by non personal means of intellectual communication or communication by teaching outside the production process itself."[6] A useful analogy might be the transmission of coded radio signals, which have marginal transmissions costs that are quite low, but where reception involves the substantial cost of constructing a receiver and decoding the information. An implication of this is that when consideration is given to both transmittal and absorption costs, the costs of transfer so defined might well be considerable, especially if the ability to decode and understand the transmitted information is not generally available.[7] The thrust of the analogy is that costs of transfer may be considerable when the recipient firm does not have the necessary skills to absorb the technology. In other words, it may be inappropriate to regard technology as something that once acquired by one firm can be made available to others at zero cost.

On a priori grounds it is difficult to assess the validity of the zero transfer cost assumption. Nevertheless, it seems to have gained wide currency, and public policy prescriptions have been predicated on its correctness.[8] It clearly seems appropriate to examine the available evidence, which unfortunately is extremely fragmentory and quite inconclusive.

Some support can be marshaled for the hypothesis that transfer costs are high. A study of the electronic capital goods industry in Britain mentions that "[t]he process known as 'Anglicisation', that is, the manufacture in Britain of American designs with some (or all) British components, can involve a considerable development effort. Several firms came to the conclusion that it would have been cheaper and quicker in some cases to design a fresh product from the start."[9] In other words, technology transfer may be more expensive than research and development on the spot, even when transfers occur between developed countries. Arrow's comments point to the same conclusion: "From the case studies, particularly those of Mueller and Peck, it can be inferred that the diffusion of information is by no means a cost free process, even apart from artificial barriers in the form of patents and secrecy . . . considerable investment must be made to make use of knowledge."[10] Mansfield seems to share this view. In his opinion:

> Economists often tended to underestimate the costs of technology transfer, that is, the cost of transferring technology from one organization to another. There was some tendency to view technology as being a stock of readily available blueprints that were usable at a nominal cost to all. The truth was that this was far from the case. For example, the U.S. decided some years back to copy a British jet engine and when the process was complete it cost more to transfer the technology than it would have to develop a new engine. Even when the problem was to transfer technology from one plant to another of the same firm the costs and headaches involved in transferring technology could be quite high.[11]

On the other hand, it seems that some economies have managed to absorb technology with very little apparent difficulty and with minimal adaptation costs. At a recent conference, E.A.G. Robinson stated that in his view, "[a]lmost the most important lesson of Hong Kong was that the conference had greatly exaggerated the cost of adapting technologies to local conditions in such a case as existed in Hong Kong."[12] While adaptation costs are not the only costs of transfer, most of the examples presented above seem to focus on this particular dimension of international technology transfer.

Further evidence is provided by the Hall and Johnson[13] study, which, although it did not present an explicit measure of transfer costs, concluded that from Japan's point of view it was more economic to transfer the technology and manufacture domestically, rather than purchase aircraft off the U.S. production lines. This is despite the very considerable advantage in learning that Lockheed had by this time acquired.

The lack of systematically collected evidence on the costs of international technology transfer is even more apparent when attention is directed to the factors that determine the level of technology transfer costs. This is especially regrettable since conceivably an identification of these factors might reconcile some of the conflicting contentions mentioned above. Nevertheless, one does sense from the literature a belief that participation in indigenous research and development is a prerequisite for success in absorbing foreign technology, and therefore is presumably a factor that will influence the cost of transfer.[14] The Japanese experience also sheds some light on this matter. In Japan:

> The import of technology was not an isolated phenomenon; parallel efforts in the form of indigenous research and development were going on in the enterprises concerned to enable them to absorb and transfer the imported technology smoothly....
> . . .
> And, in fact, many imported technologies have been improved after introduction into Japan and in the case of some of the technologies they were commercialized for the first time in the world in Japan.[15]

It is important to note that much of the technology imported into Japan was highly "advanced," and in some cases had not been previously commercialized. Although the indigenous research and development proceeded concurrent with the import of technology, it is not at all clear that it was in fact necessary for the absorption of the technology, although it was undoubtedly important for achieving further advances in the technology. In addition, the level of research and development expenditures must be kept in perspective. Some available data shows that not only were the research and development costs associated with modifying and perfecting technology only a small percentage of plant layout and production engineering costs, but they were also lower for imported technology than for indigenous technology.

In summary, the literature on the level and determinants of technology transfer costs is not only sparse; it is often confusing and contradictory. Part of the confusion stems from the fact that many of the studies do not define what is meant by 'costs of transfer,' and therefore it is not clear whether the statements are referring to the same or a different concept of technology transfer costs. Indeed, the concept of technology transfer itself is rarely defined at all carefully, either at the conceptual or the operational level. It may be that the apparent contradictions are reconcilable, since transfer costs may be higher under some circumstances than under others. However, any possible reconciliation is likely to be predicated on an understanding of the determinants of transfer costs, a topic upon which few have been prepared to even speculate.

Given the current state of inquiry, it is not surprising to find calls for research on these matters. A recent UNCTAD report suggested:

> An examination of the factors which influence the level and trends of costs of each of the elements of know-how involved in technology transfer. . . . it is not clear whether the cost differentials in the transfer of technology for similar industries in various developing countries are related to the level of development of the country and/or to the organizational form (direct investment, joint venture, or semi-public or public enterprise) employed in the transfer process.[16]

The same report also noted: "An identification of the costs and the factors which influence them. . . . would furnish a meaningful basis

Table 1-1.   Research and Development and Plant Layout Expenditures for New Products and Processes, Japan 1957-1962 (expenditures in millions of yen)

	Indigenous Technology	*Imported Technology*
Research and Development (x)	24.9	12.8
Plant layout and Production Engineering (y)	126.6	175.0
x/y for indigenous technology =	0.19	
x/y for imported technology =	0.07	

Source: M.I.T.I., Gijutsu Dohkoh Chosa Hohkolusho [Report on the Trend of Technology] (Tokyo: M.I.T.I., 1963).

for the consideration of national and international policies to reduce them."

I.4 SCOPE OF THE STUDY

In order to delineate the scope of this study, it is useful to identify two basic types of technology transfer: horizontal transfer and vertical transfer. Vertical transfer refers to the transfer of technical information within the various stages of a particular innovative process.[17] Horizontal transfer refers to the transfer of technical information from one project to another. Thus, the transfer of technical information from the basic research stage to the applied research stage of a project would be an example of vertical transfer. The transfer from one firm to another of the manufacturing technology relating to a previously commercialized[18] product or process would represent a horizontal transfer. Sometimes a transfer may involve transfers of information that are both vertical and horizontal, such as when a new product or process developed within one firm is first commercialized within another. Nevertheless, it seems useful to retain the distinction between the two basic types, since most transfers fall into either one or the other of these categories.

A further distinction can be made between three phases of horizontal technology transfer:[19] materials transfer, design transfer and capacity transfer. The first phase is characterized by the importation of new products or materials with no adaptation to the local environment. The second phase of the transfer involves the transfer of the capability to manufacture the product domestically, or in the case of process technology, to utilize the process domestically. This will involve the transmittal and absorption of the requisite technical information and skills. The third phase involves the transfer of scientific knowledge and the capability to develop new technology. This will involve the capability to modify imported technology and to develop indigenous technology. The transfer of the requisite capability could well involve the inmigration of scientists and engineers for considerable periods of time.

The domain of this study is restricted to horizontal transfers falling into the design phase as defined above. The transfers occur via firms that are multinational in the scope of their manufacturing activity. Restricting the study to this somewhat narrow domain means that other aspects of technology transfer, such as the transfer of the capability to perform research, development and engineering, are not part of this study. Nevertheless these are areas of great concern, especially to the importers of technology.[20]

Within the boundaries indicated above, this study seeks to examine the mechanics of international corporate technology transfer and to provide evidence on the level and determinants of technology transfer costs. As will become apparent in the next chapter, a rather precise "resource cost" definition of costs is employed. Externalities and the rents accruing from royalty payments are largely excluded, although some data and results on royalties will be presented by way of contrast. The focus of the study is limited to transfers both outward from and inward to but one country: the U.S.A. The transferors are corporations, generally U.S. multinational corporations. The study covers a range of corporate transfers, including the licensing of technology to independent corporations and to governments, to joint ventures and to wholly owned subsidiaries. It does not include the transfer of technology that might occur, for instance, through the export of capital goods. Although the empirical base of the study is restricted to U.S. corporations, there seems to be little evidence to suggest that corporate transfers under any other flag are substantially different in technical procedure. Furthermore, while the main focus of attention is on international technology transfer, the analysis will also highlight features common to transfers that are domestic in scope.

I.5 METHODOLOGY

Given the absolute paucity of published data on technology transfer costs as defined above, it was found necessary to obtain data by requesting it directly from multinational corporations having activities in the U.S. A sample of companies was selected, over half of which were in the chemical industry. Over 100 corporations were contacted and over 50 of these were interviewed, most of them several times. Usable data on 29 international technology transfer projects were procured. The companies that did not provide data claimed either that it did not exist or that it was proprietary and could not be made available. Nevertheless, those that could not provide data were often willing to discuss their experience with international transfers, and this information was useful for development of hypotheses and for developing the model of the anatomy of transfer found in Chapter Two.

Questionnaires were used to expedite the data collection. Since accounting systems are not generally designed to supply data in the form requested, the available data often had to be adjusted. This was always done with the assistance of groups within the firm. Sometimes parties abroad were also contacted. The foreign currency costs of the various project activities and items of equipment were converted to U.S. dollars using the exchange rate prevailing at the time the technology transfer project commenced. Although this may not be the best method of measuring the quantities of resources used in a transfer, information on prices was not known in sufficient detail to value the resources of each country in the prices of another. In any case, technology transfer decisions are generally made on the basis of cost estimates from different countries that have been pooled by converting at the exchange rate.

Part of the study involves the analysis of executives' best estimates of the quantitative effects of changes in certain variables. Data generated in this manner are not necessarily "softer" than accounting data which have been collected for quite another purpose. In any case, the conclusions of the study do not rest entirely on such data. Accounting data and executives' estimates are used in a mutually supportive manner and provide valuable checks for consistency.

I.6 THE SAMPLE

Tables 1-2—1-9 contain statistics describing some characteristics of the sample. Information on specific cases and the identity of companies has not been presented, since assurances of confidentiality were given to the respondents.[21] However, it can be seen that the transferors were on average large, experienced and fairly research-intensive enterprises. The transferees were on average much smaller, less experienced and less research-intensive. Over half of them were wholly owned subsidiaries of the transferor.

The technology transferred had generally been previously commercialized, but it cannot be thought of as "old" technology, since on average less than four years had elapsed from the first commercialization or startup to the end of the technology transfer project. The transfers can also be thought of as being fairly complete in the sense that performance is generally on a par with the parent plant performance where a parent plant does in fact exist. In some cases performance characteristics are superior to the home plant, and in others they are inferior. However, in every case the respondents felt that the transfers were complete,[22] unless there were new improvements to the technology that were being transferred on an ongoing basis. Improvements might be transferred in both directions.

Table 4-1 indicates the distribution of transfers according to the International Standard Industrial Classification (ISIC).[23] Industrial chemicals are the dominant manufacturing group, but there is a significant representation of contrasting technologies. There is con-

Table 1-2.   Characteristics of Transferor and Transferee

	Sales ($ millions)	Variable Research and Development*	Manufacturing Experience (years)
Mean			
Transferor	2,412	3.66	42.20
Transferee	604	1.74	14.06
Std Deviation			
Transferor	5,185	2.50	30.20
Transferee	1,391	2.33	16.82
Maximum			
Transferor	20,000	12.50	100.00
Transferee	5,000	10.00	50.00
Minimum			
Transferor	1.00	1.20	4.00
Transferee	0	0	1.00
Sample Size			
Transferor	29	29	29
Transferee	29	29	29

*Research and development expenditures as a percentage of sales value.

Table 1-3.   Ownership of Transferee

Form	Number of Cases
Wholly owned subsidiary of transferor	15
Joint venture with transferor	8
Wholly independent private enterprise	4
Government enterprises	3
	29

Table 1-4.   Some Characteristics of the Technology

	Mean	Standard Deviation	Maximum	Minimum	N
Age (years)	6.34	7.60	30.0	1.0	29
Number of previous manufacturing startups	3.58	4.18	14.0	0	29
Number of firms	5.82	6.15	20.0	0	29
Time taken for transfer (months)	35.68	19.50	92.0	12.0	25

Table 1-5. Perceived Performance Characteristics of Foreign Plant Compared to Home Plant

	Higher	*Lower*	*Same*	N
Labor productivity	3	6	17	26
Materials efficiency	2	2	22	26
Quality of output	0	1	25	26

Table 1-6. Geographical Location of Transferee

Location	*Number of Transfers*
North America	3
Northern and Western Europe	11
Australia	1
Japan	4
Eastern Europe	2
Latin America	5
Asia (excluding Japan)	2
Africa	1
Total	29

Table 1-7. Distribution of Transfers According to Date Transfers Commenced

Year	*Number of Transfers*
1960-1965	5
1966-1970	11
1970-1975	13
	29

Table 1-8. GNP Per Capita,* 1971 (U.S. dollars), of Host Countries in Sample (weighted by number of transfers to host country)

Mean	*Standard Deviation*	*Maximum*	*Minimum*
2,245	1,317	5,160	290

*Source of GNP per capita statistics: *World Bank Atlas* (Washington, D.C.: International Bank for Reconstruction and Development, 1973).

Table 1-9.   Industrial Classification of Transfers by Three and Four Digit ISIC Code

ISIC Code		Title of Category	Number of Transfers	
Three digit	Four digit			
351		Manufacture of industrial chemicals		(16)
	3511	Manufacture of basic industrial chemicals except fertilizers	10	
	3513	Synthetic resins, plastics materials and man made fibres except glass	4	
	3521	Manufacture of paints, varnishes and lacquers	2	
353	3530	Petroleum refineries	3	(3)
356	3560	Manufacture of plastics products not elsewhere identified	1	(1)
381		Manufacture of fabricated metal products, machinery and equipment		(1)
	3819	Manufacture of fabricated metal products except machinery and equipment not elsewhere classified	1	
382		Manufacture of machinery except electrical		(5)
	3825	Manufacture of office, computing and accounting machinery	3	
	3829	Manufacture of machinery and equipment except electrical not elsewhere classified	2	
383		Manufacture of electrical machinery apparatus, appliances and supplies		(3)
	3831	Manufacture of electrical industrial machinery and apparatus	2	
	3832	Manufacture of radio, TV and communication equipment and apparatus	1	
				(29)

Table 1-10. Cross-Classification of ISIC Category and Transferee Location

Location	*Three digit ISIC code*						
	351	*353*	*356*	*381*	*382*	*383*	
North America	1	1	0	1	0	0	3
Northern and Western Europe	5	1	0	0	4	1	11
Australia	0	0	1	0	0	0	1
Japan	3	0	0	0	1	0	4
Eastern Europe	2	0	0	0	0	0	2
Latin America	4	0	0	0	0	1	5
Asia (excluding Japan)	0	1	0	0	0	1	2
Africa	1	0	0	0	0	0	1
	16	3	1	1	5	3	29

siderable dispersion in the location and income levels of the host countries, but there does not seem to be any obvious correlation between this and the industry classification. It would seem that although the sample is small, there is nothing to prevent its being used in a preliminary study of the costs of international technology transfer, so long as it is remembered that the sample is unlikely to be typical of more than a very limited class of transfers. Unfortunately, this study had to depend on the data that participating firms were prepared to make available, and it was not possible to exercise any kind of selectivity over the projects examined. There was, however, a definite bias toward projects for which the data were relatively easily accessible. This often implied that the transfers were quite recent (see Table 1.7).

NOTES

1. For a discussion of the technology gap see D.L. Spencer, *Technology Gap in Perspective* (New York: Spartan Books, 1970).
2. Simon Kuznets, *Modern Economic Growth: Rate, Structure, and Spread* (New Haven: Yale University Press, 1966), p. 287.
3. Kenneth Arrow, "Classifactory Notes on the Production and Transmission of Technological Knowledge," *American Economic Review, Papers and Proceedings* 59:33 (May 1969).
4. See for example, Lloyd Reynolds, "Discussion," *American Economic Review* 56:112-14 (May 1966).
5. For a recent example of this see C.A. Rodriguez, "Trade in Technical Knowledge and the National Advantage," *Journal of Political Economy*

83:121-35 (February 1975). In his model "[t]ransmission of technology is assumed costless. Thus, it is possible for the country which owns the technology to operate a plant in a foreign country without any transfer of factors" (p. 122).

6. I. Svennilson, *Economic Development with Special Reference to East Asia*, K. Berrill, ed. (New York: St. Martin's Press, 1964), p. 407.

7. Rosenberg is "impressed by the extent to which the transfer of technological skills—even between two countries so apparently 'close together' as Britain and the United States in the mid-19th century—was dependent upon the transfer of skilled personnel." See N. Rosenberg, "Economic Development and the Transfer of Technology: Some Historical Perspectives," *Technology and Culture* 11:553 (October 1970).

8. For two separate but identical prescriptions, see W. Leontief, "On Assignments of Patent Rights on Inventions Made Under Government Research Contracts," *Harvard Law Review* 77:492 (January 1964); and H.G. Johnson, "The Efficiency and Welfare Implications of the International Corporation," in C.P. Kindleberger, ed., *The International Corporation* (Cambridge: M.I.T. Press, 1970), p. 36. These prescriptions are correct only if it is assumed that the transferee pays the appropriate transfer fees.

9. See C. Freeman, "Research and Development in Electronic Capital Goods," *National Institute Economic Review* 34:63 (November 1965).

10. K. Arrow, "Comment," in Universities—National Bureau Committee for Economic Research, *The Rate and Direction of Inventive Activity* (Princeton: Princeton University Press, 1962), p. 354.

11. E. Mansfield, "Discussion of the Paper by Professor Griliches," in B.R. Williams, ed., *Science and Technology in Economic Growth* (New York: John Wiley, 1973), p. 90.

12. E.A.G. Robinson, "Discussion of the Paper by Professor Hsia," in B.R. Williams, ed., *Science and Technology in Economic Growth* (New York: John Wiley, 1973), p. 355.

13. G.R. Hall and R.D. Johnson, "Transfers of United States Aerospace Technology to Japan," in R. Vernon, ed., *The Technology Factor in International Trade* (New York: National Bureau of Economic Research, 1970), p. 305.

14. See, for example, C. Freeman, "Discussion of the Paper by Professor Trickovic," In B.R. Williams, ed., *Science and Technology in Economic Growth* (New York: John Wiley, 1973), p. 304.

15. K. Oshima, "Research and Development and Economic Growth in Japan," in B.R. Williams, ed., *Science and Technology in Economic Growth* (New York: John Wiley, 1973), p. 317.

16. UNCTAD, "The Transfer of Technology," *Journal of World Trade Law* 4:711 (September-October 1970).

17. For a description of the stages of the product innovation process, see E. Mansfield et al., *Research and Innovation in the Modern Corporation* (New York: W.W. Norton, 1971), ch. 6.

18. An innovation is said to have been commercialized if it has already been applied in a facility of economic size that is essentially nonexperimental in nature. Thus, pilot plant or prototype application is not considered to represent commercialization.

19. These phases are distinguished by Y. Hayami and V. Ruttan, *Agricultural Development and International Perspective* (Baltimore: Johns Hopkins, 1971), p. 175.

20. See, for example, National Academy of Sciences, *U.S. International Firms and R, D, and E in Developing Countries* (Washington, D.C., 1973).

21. The Appendix contains a description of each of the 29 transfers included in the data base.

22. "Completeness" as used here does not imply that the degree of value added established abroad is identical to the degree of value added existent in domestic operations. Rather, it is the degree to which the productivity, materials efficiency and product quality of a given dimension of the technology is successfully transferred abroad. For example, if an assembling operation only is transferred, then assembly operations abroad and at home are compared with respect to the above characteristics.

23. For definitions of the categories, see United Nations, *International Standard Industrial Classification of all Economic Activities*, United Nations Statistical Papers, series M, no. 4 (New York, 1968).

Chapter Two

The Anatomy of International Technology Transfer

II.1 INTRODUCTION

Although case studies have been made of the process by which technology is transferred from one enterprise to another, these studies have made little attempt to identify procedures that are common to many different kinds of technology transfer. While recognizing the diversity in international technology transfer, one of the objectives of this study is to point to procedures that are indeed common to many cases of technology transfer. In addition, this chapter aims to highlight aspects of the international transfer of technology that distinguish it in character from domestic technology transfer: that is, the technology transfer that occurs from enterprise to enterprise within the nation state. Further, the concept of technology transfer itself is reviewed. In particular, the choice between the internal development of technology and technology transfer is examined, with special emphasis on the international dimensions of the problem. Finally, a workable definition of transfer costs is presented.

II.2 THE DIVERSITY IN INTERNATIONAL TECHNOLOGY TRANSFER

Technology transfer was defined in Chapter One as the process of transferring from one production entity to another the know-how required to successfully utilize a particular technology. While a general statement of this kind is suggestive of the subject matter of this study, it fails to highlight the enormous diversity in the type and nature of technology transfer that actually takes place. So great is the diversity that many businessmen and engineers interviewed in this study were skeptical that a cross-section study could possibly make any sense of the diversity of real world transfer activity.

While realizing that any study based on a small sample is at best suggestive, it behooves the social scientist to at least attempt to see order in the real world, and to search for patterns, causes and effects. Indeed, the excellence of a social scientist is measured not so much by his ability to give the most detailed possible description of the real world, although description may be instructive, but to search for underlying patterns, and the factors that might be responsible for the patterns that are observed.

Despite the limitations on subject matter defined in Chapter One, it is important to realize that there is still a great diversity in the projects that have been included under the umbrella of international technology transfer. The most clear-cut example is when manufacturing ability is transferred to an area where no previous manufacturing has taken place. Managers refer to this as a "green fields" transfer, and a "grass roots" operation will have to be conducted to insure the success of the transfer. A new plant will have to be built and the labor force trained, and much of the supporting infrastructure may have to be created as well: e.g., roads, electricity, telephone and other utilities. Projects in less-developed countries may approach the "green fields" situation. Clearly, it will impose formidable but not insurmountable barriers to the transfer of technology. Large inputs of resources both local and imported will have to be provided. This will be especially true if the contemplated production facility is to be fully integrated, rather than merely an assembling or finishing facility. In many cases, a transfer such as the one just described is likely to proceed on a piecemeal basis if technological possibilities exist for disaggregating the production process. For example, consider the transfer of electrical goods. Assembly operations may be transferred first, and component manufacture may follow as the market expands and the transferee gains more experience. For a continuous flow technology, possibilities for disaggregation may not exist. In the chemical industry, for instance, there may be large heat losses or material wastage if disaggregation is attempted.

Most examples of technology transfer probably do not fall into the "green fields" category. Many examples can be found where a new product or a new process is merely introduced into an existing enterprise that already has some manufacturing experience, perhaps in the industry to which the new process or product belongs. Any enterprise that has had success in manufacturing is likely to have acquired certain general skills, both technical and managerial, that are likely to be of use in whatever new venture it decides to embark upon. Hence, the nature of the transfer under these circumstances is likely to be different from the nature of the transfer described above. The problems of transfer will be eased very considerably, particularly if the transferee has had experience in very similar manufacturing endeavors. An enterprise that has previously manufactured typewriters will clearly have less trouble including sewing machines in its product line than it would have including vinyl chloride. Indeed, it may be possible to use the existing plant and perhaps some of the existing tooling for the new venture.

Other examples of technology transfer may merely involve the introduction of new models or new families of models into an enterprise already acquainted with the basic technology of a particular industry. In these cases, much of the existing tooling as well as the existing plant can be utilized for the new venture. The labor force is likely to be quite familiar with the basic technology involved.

II.3 INTERNATIONAL TECHNOLOGY TRANSFER AND THE INTERNAL DEVELOPMENT OF TECHNOLOGY

Technology transfer represents the expression of a choice to "import" technology rather than to develop it within the firm. There are good reasons why many innovations are "imported" rather than developed internally. One might be that the firm is part of a worldwide network of research and development and manufacturing facilities; specialization would then imply importation from other parts of the corporation of at least certain types of innovations. This scenario fits the circumstance of a subsidiary of a multinational corporation. Indeed, several studies suggest that direct foreign investment by U.S. corporations is based on the exploitation of innovations.[1] However, many cases of technology transfer do not occur within the multinational corporation. Various explanations can be advanced to suggest why transfers occur to independent corporations. From the buyer's point of view, it is clear that transfer is often the least expensive method of acquiring access to an innovation. In addition, technology transfer is perhaps the lowest risk route to the acquisition of technical ability and excellence in manufacturing. When a firm buys a license to an already commercialized innovation, it is buying low risk access to new products or superior processes.

The international transfer of technology that has not been commercialized occurs rather infrequently; when it does occur, it generally takes place within the multinational firm. One reason is that it is difficult to convince potential licensees of the innate value of the technology. This is essentially a market failure problem. The fixing of a price for information is a difficult exercise, since one really needs the information to decide what price one is willing to pay, and this is an inherent impossibility with the market for proprietary knowledge. The fixing of prices for technology therefore takes place partly in ignorance from the point of view of both parties. The other main reason why the transfer of technology that has not been previously commercialized occurs infrequently might be a technical reason; the problems encountered in separating first production from development can be quite formidable because of the extent of the information flow required. Constant contact will be needed between development groups at home and production groups abroad. Elongating the lines of communication at the development interface will add considerably to the costs of transfer. The risk of failure and cost overruns is likely to be high under these circumstances.

Nevertheless, the separation by international boundaries of first production from development is feasible, at least in some cases, but relatively large transfer costs may be involved. Measurement of the magnitude of these transfer costs has not been attempted in any previous studies of international transfer or domestic transfer, although there is recognition that even for domestic transfers the costs of separating first production from development might be high.[2] Because of the extra costs generally involved, it is not likely that transfers of this nature will take place unless there is a compelling marketing motivation.

II.4 DIFFERENCES BETWEEN DOMESTIC AND INTERNATIONAL TECHNOLOGY TRANSFER

Although this is a study of international technology transfer, it is quite apparent that many of the characteristics of international technology transfer are also characteristic of the technology transfer that occurs within national borders. For instance, one may ask whether there is any difference between transferring technology from Pennsylvania to California and transferring technology from Pennsylvania to the United Kingdom. While admittedly there are cases where international boundaries do not represent any significant barrier, there are generally some quite important differences to which attention should be drawn.

First, with international transfer, the problems associated with the acceptance of external or "imported" technology are likely to be accentuated. A very common problem encountered with technology transfer is the "not invented here" syndrome. Ideas originating from outside the firm may be despised if they displace or threaten ideas that have been generated internally. Further, even if the need for the innovation is accepted, divergent viewpoints may arise in the course of the transfer as to how the transfer should proceed. The transferee is prone to believe that since it will have prime responsibility for operating the technology, its viewpoints should be given preeminence with respect to the transfer procedure. The transferor, on the other hand, is likely to feel that since it developed the technology and probably also brought it to commercialization, it is in a far better position to guide the transfer than is the transferee. Natural suspicions and pride are likely to be accentuated if the parties are of different nationalities. Although these problems can be reduced if management works for an early consensus at all levels on the need for the transfer and the best method of conducting it, it is still likely that international transfers will entail more problems of this kind than will domestic transfers.

Second, the need for adaptation of the technology to local conditions is likely to be greater if the technology is transferred internationally. There are many reasons why adaptation may be necessary. The size of the foreign market is likely to be different from the size of the domestic market. If the domestic market is the U.S.A., then the size difference is most marked when technology is transferred to less developed countries. Considerable scaling down in the size of the plant will be necessary unless production is for the world market. Successful scale alternation can provide a considerable engineering challenge. If possible, the technology needs to be scaled so as to preserve the advantages of the macro technology without installing excess capacity. Despite the difficulties, the extent to which successful scale adaptation is possible is sometimes amazing. For example, one U.S. company manufacturing synthetic fibers operated an optimum size plant of 400 million pounds in the U.S. They managed to scale this down to a seven million pound plant for their Latin American joint venture while still using most of the elements of its most advanced technology with great success. Nevertheless, there may be cases where the scaling down of modern technology cannot be achieved; in these cases, "intermediate"[3] technology may be more appropriate if the scale requirements are less demanding. The need for adaptation also arises because of international differences in factor prices. Factor prices are unlikely to vary much within a nation because of factor mobility; but amongst nations, immobility of some factors is likely to induce differences in factor costs. In order to achieve least cost production, adaptation may be necessary. This will impose further engineering challenges; it may turn out that adaptation will cost more than the potential savings through reduced production costs. Some production processes may offer little in the way of capital-labor substitution. For instance, with many capital-intensive processes, the technology is embodied in the plant and equipment. At most, some reduction in peripheral equipment may be possible. For instance, in a low labor cost country, bulk handling can be replaced by bags and drums. Another motivation for adaptation is that there are larger differences in skills between nations than there are within nations. Hence, any adaptation to the technology that can simplify its operations is likely to be attempted if the return seems worthwhile. This kind of adaptation will permit less exposure to human error and minimization of the deleterious consequences of error. For example, it may be possible to engineer a low risk design for a chemical plant by providing excess capacity in the furnaces and by providing emergency power supplies in case of failure in the national grid. It is also possible to engineer so that maintenance is kept as simple as possible. Sometimes requirements such as these can add to the total cost of the plant quite considerably. Adaptation of the product itself may sometimes also be desired. International markets are generally less homogeneous than domestic markets, so unless the final product is for reexport to the home country, some adaptation of the product may seem desirable. However, a countervailing concern may be the need for standardization, particularly when technology transfer takes place to a subsidiary. Worldwide standardization and quality control may be sought to facilitate the interchangeability of parts; but such standardization is not always possible. One company manufacturing measuring devices used in the chemical industry discovered that in some European oil refineries and chemical plants there is a much greater use of flanges than screws. The product design had to be adapted accordingly. A further and rather obvious reason for adaptation is international differences in units of measurement and engineering standards. If the home country uses ASA sizes, and the host country uses DIN sizes, adaptation will be necessary. Conversion to metric and vice versa may also be necessary. Although each change may involve a trivial cost, the aggregate cost may not be trivial.[4]

A third source of differences between international and domestic transfer is that conducting the former often involves confronting large differences in infrastructure between home and host locations. Some of the sources of difference have already been alluded to, such as differences in skills, factor prices and availability of utilities. However, there are also major differences in the cultural and legal milieu in which businesses must operate. Management procedures that have proved successful at home may be unacceptable where attitudes and values are different. Further, there may be a plethora of government controls that the venture must consider. For example, in the drug industry, approvals and clearances represent the greatest cost associated with drug production and marketing abroad. Many governments will not accept clinical data generated from outside the country. Repeating the testing could cost millions of dollars.

Distance and communication costs are a fourth group of factors differentiating international from domestic transfers. Although the communications revolution of the twentieth century has enormously reduced the barrier of distance,[5] the costs of international communications are not insignificant. For example, one U.S. company estimated that travel, telegraph, freight and insurance added about 10 percent to the total cost of a project established in New Zealand. Further, if it had not been for distance, the cost of the plant would have been almost identical to the U.S. cost. Language differences can be another important element of communication costs, especially if the translation of engineering drawings is required. This statement is corroborated by the experience of a U.K. firm, Polyspinners Ltd., and contractor John Brown, when they established a £40 million synthetic fiber complex in the USSR. The project manager stated:

> Once we agreed on a drawing in Moscow, we had to get it back to London, for translation and printing. Printing in two languages that is; with 8 copies for the Russians—texts and schedules. At peak periods every competent freelance translator or agency in the U.K. was being used in addition to our own department of about 30 people.[6]

The project manager estimated that documentation alone cost £500,000 and the translation a similar amount. There are other indirect costs that are difficult to measure; for instance, the misunderstanding of instructions could result in mistakes that are costly to correct.

II.5 MODES AND METHODS OF TRANSFER

Another interesting dimension of the process of international technology transfer is the variety of modes via which the technology may be transferred. It may, for instance, be transferred within the multinational corporation, from parent to subsidiary and vice versa, or from subsidiary to subsidiary. On the other hand, it may be transferred from a corporation to another completely independent enterprise, or to an enterprise in which the transferor has some equity interest: i.e., a joint venture. Various hypotheses have been advanced as to why one mode might be preferred over another.[7] However, with respect to understanding the mechanics of transfer, it is of equal importance to understand variation in the procedure or methods of transfer. Two classes of transfer can be distinguished: internal transfer and "arms length" market-mediated transfer. In the former, the transfer interface is contained within the recipient and donor; in the latter, an intermediary, generally an engineering contractor, is also at the interface, and transactions proceed strictly according to the latter model.

The role of the engineering contractor and the construction contractor in international technology transfer seems to deserve some attention. Contractors are important actors in the technology transfer, irrespective of whether the transfer is by direct investment or by licensing to an independent enterprise. Although the role of the contractors will change from industry to industry and from circumstance to circumstance, they will generally be responsible for the engineering of the plant, plant construction, and the engineering for some key pieces of equipment. In some market-mediated transfers they may also arrange the buying and selling of the technology. Although skills will have to be brought to bear during all of these activities, the skills are those of the engineering industry rather than skills relating to the production technology.

There are various reasons why engineering and construction contractors are engaged by the parties to the transfer. An obvious reason is specialization. The donors and recipients of technology are primarily manufacturing entities and not engineering and technology transfer agencies. They perceive their prime function to be specialization in production and not engineering and construction, although they may have some capabilities in these areas. Hence, there is a desire to hand over to contractors as much of the project responsibilities as possible. Further, if a contractor in the host country can be engaged, it is likely to be familiar with the local environment: the regulations, codes and systems of measurement peculiar to a particular country. A second reason why engineering and construction contractors are engaged is simply that few companies are large enough to support teams to engineer and construct their own plants. Most firms have fairly limited in-house engineering facilities.

Nevertheless, there are some transfers that do not proceed through engineering and construction contractors. These may represent cases of market failure. Party-to-party transfers may occur when problems of secrecy are paramount, or when a basic engineering or "process package" does not exist. If a process package does not exist, then it is very difficult for the contractor to understand the technology. The need for secrecy and the lack of a process package are often characteristic of technology that has not yet been commercialized. When the technology has not been commercialized, engineering changes will occur frequently and most contractors are generally not capable of handling such changes willingly or effectively. The problem may be somewhat eased if contractors are engaged in cost plus contracts, but transferors are generally reluctant to arrange contracts of this type. If it has the facilities, a transferor will prefer to do the engineering in-house rather than risk a cost plus contract. Market failure is in this case a result of the pairing of uncertainty and bounded rationality.[8] Because of limits on man's ability to receive, store, retrieve and process information, it is costly or impossible to identify future contingencies and to specify appropriate adaptations *ex ante*. Accordingly, contracts may be supplanted by internal organization, since recourse to in-house engineering permits adaptations to technological uncertainty to be accomplished by administrative processes as each problem arises. Internal organization therefore economizes on the bounded rationality of decisionmakers where uncertainty is substantial.

Although much of the above discussion of the role of the contractor is particularly relevant to the transfer of process technology, similar relationships hold for the transfer of product technology. A contractor will almost always be engaged to perform whatever civil engineering is required, but the manufacturing engineering is likely to be done by the transferor unless it is of a routine nature. This is because a good deal of firm-specific and system-specific information is embodied in the manufacturing engineering (see Section II.9).

An interesting further dimension to the "who performs what" aspect of international technology transfer is the division of the remaining functions between transferor and transferee. Generally, the transferor performs a good deal of the transfer activities, and this seems consistent with general notions of technology transfer. However, the transferee can never escape the learning activities required to absorb the technology. Nevertheless, there are circumstances where the transferor performs very little at all. This might be because foreign operations or licensing are marginal to its activities—the result of a take it or leave it attitude to the licensing of technology—or it might simply be a reflection of only very small information asymmetries between transferor and transferee.[9] In general, however, technology transfer is characterized by large information asymmetries between transferor and transferee.

II.6 STAGES IN TECHNOLOGY TRANSFER PROJECTS[10]

The decision to transfer technology will typically follow months of information collection and evaluation. Once the decision to go ahead with the transfer is made, a set of well-defined activities will have to be performed. It is the performance of these activities that results in technology transfer. Four major and one preliminary stage in the transfer process can be identified. These stages occur sequentially, although there will generally be some overlap. Each involves a resource commitment of a quite different character from the preceding stage. The stages also involve changes in the level of resource commitment by recipient and by donor. However, the basic mechanics are sufficiently invariant under a variety of circumstances to make a general description meaningful.

Preinvestment or Feasibility Study

The path to transfer begins when a need or a potential is recognized, and a feasibility study is conducted to determine if a project is acceptable on some criteria, for example, profitability. Where profitability is to be the criteria of acceptance, the feasibility study is likely to include a marketing analysis, materials and labor availability analysis, and technological assessment. The analysis will be predicated on certain performance assumptions concerning the technology that is to be utilized. Several feasibility studies may be conducted utilizing different locations and different performance data on different technologies. The studies may take several years. Very often a management consulting firm will be hired to prepare the analysis. Regardless of who conducts the feasibility study, it may involve a considerable commitment of resources over many months, especially if the contemplated investment is very large. Consider a technology transfer project/involving the establishment of a metal ore smelter. Exhaustive studies will first have to be conducted to discover the extent and quality of the ore deposit, the best way to mine it and the appropriate facilities for transporting it to the smelter. Another group of studies will deal with the location of the smelter. The economics will be evaluated on the basis of the cost factors ruling in different locations. All of these considerations, assumptions and calculations are summarized in the feasibility study, which then serves as the basis for evaluation of the project.

If preliminary estimates indicate that the project is potentially profitable, the next step is likely to involve solicitation of bids for various elements of the engineering and plant construction. Solicitation of bids for access to a suitable technology may also occur if the initiative for the transfer is coming from the potential transferee. In cases where a parent firm is to supply the technology, then this step will be bypassed.

When a licensing agreement has to be reached, a protracted period of bargaining may ensue. Considerable selling expense may accrue to the licensor, particularly if the potential licensee is a government enterprise, or if it does not have a great deal of technical or managerial expertise. Several transferors claimed that their direct costs for a single contract sometimes ran over $100,000 with no guarantee that a license would be consummated.[11] Weeks of technical discussions and contract bargaining might be required. All of this would take place in the host country at considerable expense to the transferor and the contractors. However, differences in selling expense may be built into the royalty payment. For this reason the cost to some firms may be different from the cost to others for identical licenses.

The transfer program generally begins in earnest once the contract is signed. If no license is involved, the transfer begins when the formal approval of the relevant executive group or groups is obtained. However, it is clear that by this time some technical knowledge might have already been transferred through the technical consultation that preceded the consummation of an agreement. Nevertheless, in the case of licensing, the necessity of maintaining a certain amount of secrecy would result in some key elements of the technology having been withheld.

Stage A

Once an agreement is consummated and the project approved, the key elements of the process or product design will be transferred. This is critical information, and top level researchers and engineers are likely to be involved. Scientific information and research results will be transferred in top level discussions amongst scientists, engineers and managers. If it happens that the transferee is already familiar with the science, then no transfer of this type of information will be necessary. This is likely if the transferee is manufacturing similar products or utilizing similar processes or if the underlying innovation is quite old.

Stage B

The second stage, hereafter Stage B, involves the engineering and design, and the planning of production. These activities are discussed, first with respect to continuous flow process technology (such as chemical and petroleum refining), and second with respect to product technology[1][2] (such as machine manufacture). With respect to the former, a distinction can be made between process engineering and detailed engineering. Process engineering involves the compilation of flow diagrams, heat balances and control instrumentation, etc. It can be distinguished from the detailed engineering that involves the translation and elaboration of the process engineering into a manufacturing facility. The detailed engineering can be rather routine and generally involves a large amount of drafting. Although supervision and consultation will be required, the drafting itself requires general engineering skills rather than skills or knowledge unique to a particular firm or process. Drawings and specifications are compiled that contain the design parameters of every piece of equipment and their delivery requirements. The layout of buildings and other facilities will be included. The drawings and specifications will be the basis for inquiries for the equipment and for plant construction.

For the international transfer of technology, considerable advantage will arise if the technology has already been commercialized. This will mean that a process engineering package or a basic engineering package will already have been assembled. Although exact duplication of this for an overseas project is unlikely to be possible, transfer will nevertheless be greatly facilitated if a package exists. However, it is rarely that a package can be effectively transferred without considerable contact between the scientists and engineers of the transferor and transferee. At the minimum, consulting services will have to be provided to help the transferee or the engineering contractor absorb the package. Large, sophisticated, experienced recipients are nevertheless able to absorb a package with surprisingly little assistance. Others may make enormous demands on support facilities. Teams of engineers may have to go abroad to ensure the successful absorption of the package.

With respect to product technology, a distinction can be made between functional design, production design and process planning. Functional design involves design of a product to fulfill certain specifications and requirements. The production design involves modification of the functional design in order to render it amenable to low cost manufacture. Given the production design, process planning must proceed to specify, in careful detail, the processes required and their sequence. The production design first sets the minimum possible cost that can be achieved through the specification of materials, tolerances and basic configurations. The accepted end point for production design is manifested by the drawing release, which summarizes the exact specifications of what is to be made. Process planning takes over from this point and develops the broad plan of manufacture for the part or product. A distinction should also be drawn between process planning and plant layout and facilities planning. Process planning blends with the layout of physical facilities. Some process planning will take place during the layout phases of the design of a production system. Process plans can be regarded as inputs to the development of a layout. When an international transfer falls into the design phase,[13] the product design is unlikely to be substantially adjusted. However, the process planning may be altered, since ordinarily the range or promising alternatives is considerable, and the selection may be influenced strongly by the overall volume and projected stability of design.

Stage C

The third stage in the transfer, hereafter Stage C, involves the construction, tooling and installation of the manufacturing facilities. This will be performed by construction contractors, and these same firms may also perform the civil engineering. The civil engineering and construction contractors will execute the project under the direction of the project manager supplied by one or other of the parties to the transfer. Although a considerable amount of know-how is needed to organize and delegate the work and responsibilities, the cost of providing this is likely to be very small relative to other expenditures. One good manager on site can provide much of the required input.

Stage D

A fourth stage, hereafter Stage D, will be termed the manufacturing startup. This is sometimes referred to in business parlance as "bringing the plant on stream." The activities involved are again very different from those in the preceding stages. The training of operatives, and the alteration, adjustment, dismantling and replacement of unsatisfactory equipment all occur during this phase. The startup training often begins before the mechanical startup of the plant. The effective training of the labor force is extremely critical for technology transfer. If the labor force already possesses basic industry skills then the training of operatives will be relatively easy; otherwise, programs for basic training will have to be implemented. Prestartup training will be needed unless operatives have skills almost commensurate with those needed for the production process. This training can be provided by the transferor sending instructional teams into the field. Considerable opportunity costs will be involved since the best operatives must be taken from the domestic operations. Alternatively, operatives from abroad can be brought into the transferor's existing plants and given on the job training. This is an expensive option and the results can be quite unsatisfactory, especially if the plants are quite different. The most effective type of training is on the job training in the actual facility; the cost here is expressed in terms of low initial productivity, high wastage of materials and temporary shutdowns. Although supervisors and consultants can be brought in to assist during the startup, there is no escape from incurring some initial losses as the operation progresses along the learning curve. The slope of the learning curve will differ from industry to industry, but there is no doubt that a well-planned and well-executed startup will propel the plant to the break even point quicker than a mismanaged startup that has to contend with supervisory and operator ignorance.

When the operation is debugged and the plant is running smoothly, the startup will end and the consultants and troubleshooters will be withdrawn. Productivity will probably still continue to improve. Clearly, the termination of the formal startup is somewhat arbitrary. The definition used in this study is that the plant is considered to be on stream when it has reached the design or expected productivity level. The losses incurred during startup can be enormous, particularly when the output of the plant is not usable. To some extent, the costs will depend on the nature of the technology, in that a technology that allows scrap to be recycled or reworked will have lower startup cost than a technology where this is no such possibility. Costs to the transferor will depend on how long the excess startup personnel have to stay in the field. If there has been poor transfer and absorption of the technology in the earlier phases, it will most likely become apparent during the startup. For instance, failure to adapt the engineering to local conditions, failure to inspect for job quality, inadequate prestartup training and low calibre management will manifest themselves in large startup cost overruns, equipment and engineering changes, and temporary shutdowns. In other words, startup costs are, *ceteris paribus*, an index of how well the technology has been transferred and absorbed.

II.7 STAGES IN INTERNATIONAL PROJECTS: COST AND TIME

The stages that have been identified involve different levels of resource commitment. Cost data were collected on Stages A, B, C and D as identified above. Table 2-1 presents a summary of this information.

It is clear from the summary statistics that by far the largest percentage of the total project costs are incurred during Stage C, which is the plant construction, the tooling and the installation of equipment. For the sample as a whole, this accounts on the average for 75 percent of the total costs. The next largest percentage of total costs for the sample as a whole occurs during Stage D, which is the manufacturing startup and accounts for 14 percent of the total cost on average. The Stage B costs, which represent the expenses of engineering and design, account for almost all of the remainder of

Table 2-1.   Descriptive Statistics on Percentage of Total Cost Arising in Each Stage of Project*

		Chemicals and Petroleum Refining**	Machinery**	Whole Sample
Stage A				
(Transfer of	minimum	0	0	0
research results	maximum	5	1	5
and design	mean	1	1	1
fundamentals)	standard deviation	1	0	1
	sample size	19	9	28
Stage B				
(Engineering and	minimum	3	1	1
design, production	maximum	22	18	22
planning)	mean	10	8	9
	standard deviation	6	6	6
	sample size	19	9	28
Stage C				
(Construction,	minimum	64	41	41
tooling and	maximum	95	90	95
installation)	mean	81	63	75
	standard deviation	8	14	13
	sample size	19	9	28
Stage D				
(Manufacturing	minimum	1	7	1
startup)	maximum	14	57	57
	mean	7	28	14
	standard deviation	4	15	13
	sample size	19	9	28

*Costs are rounded to nearest percentage. Total project cost corresponds here and elsewhere with the inside boundary limits definition commonly used by project accountants. The sum of Stages A, B, C and D is equal to total project cost.

**Chemicals and Petroleum Refining includes projects in ISIC categories 3511, 3513, 3521, 3530, 3560. Machinery includes the projects in ISIC 3819, 3825, 3829, 3831, 3832 (see Table 1-9 of this study).

the total cost. Stage A costs are almost negligible, indicating that in most cases very little resources were applied to transferring the results of applied research and the design fundamentals. This is consistent with the observation that many transfers involve the transfer of already developed and previously tried and tested technology, so that relatively minor activity in applied research is involved.

Table 2-2 shows the distribution of time over the various stages of the project. The elapsed time for a given stage includes the overlap with adjacent stages. Stage times do not follow a pattern identical to stage costs. There is a significant amount of time devoted to the Stage A activities. In view of the relatively minor expenses incurred, it is necessary to conclude that Stage A activity involves minimal

Table 2-2. Descriptive Statistics on Percentage of Total Time Arising in Each Stage* of Project

		Chemicals and Petroleum Refining	Machinery	Whole Sample
Stage A				
(Transfer of	minimum	0	0	0
research results	maximum	60	42	60
and design	mean	18	7	14
fundamentals)	standard deviation	18	15	17
	sample size	16	8	24
Stage B				
(Engineering and	minimum	8	5	5
design, production	maximum	64	77	77
planning)	mean	30	40	33
	standard deviation	17	26	20
	sample size	17	8	25
Stage C				
(Construction,	minimum	5	21	5
tooling and	maximum	73	45	73
installation)	mean	47	34	43
	standard deviation	19	8	17
	sample size	17	8	25
Stage D				
(Manufacturing	minimum	2	13	2
startup)	maximum	38	57	57
	mean	12	38	20
	standard deviation	8	18	17
	sample size	16	8	23

*The duration of a given stage, here and elsewhere, includes the overlaps with adjacent stages. The data is rounded to the nearest percent.

resource commitment but considerable delays. Indeed, this is the phase when discussions take place on the basic design parameters. The most appropriate manner to proceed with the transfer will also be mapped out by management. In contrast to Stage A, Stage C is a phase of concentrated activity as a diverse set of resources are assembled and applied. Stages B and D account for the remainder of the time. There is often a considerable difference between the distribution of costs and time for the industry groupings identified. Of particular note is the relatively high level of startup cost and startup time incurred in the machinery category. This may reflect the significant learning economics available, and the costs of attaining them.

II.8 DEPARTURES FROM THE SIMPLE STAGE MODEL

Although it is appropriate to present the above generalized description, it is necessary to note that there will always be some deviations from the general model, particularly if the project is very small. For instance, the feasibility study might be quite informal, and the engineering may not proceed in the well-structured manner suggested. Indeed, it is possible that no engineering drawings may be transferred at all. Sometimes the transfer of product technology can take place entirely through the transfer of samples. The samples are shipped and dismantled, and drawings are made of each component. The transferee then proceeds to attempt to manufacture the product, sometimes with no assistance from the transferor. The transferee must have a certain level of skill and systems ability before this approach is likely to be successful. However, it is not uncommon for samples to be sent along with a few technical support personnel.[14] A similar procedure for the transfer of process technology is frequently observed. The diffusion of British textile technology to France in the nineteenth century also proceeded in this manner.[15] Key pieces of equipment were smuggled out of Britain to continental Europe. Many machines could be copied from a single model. It was also necessary to secure the services of a few highly skilled artisans who could train French workers to handle the new machines. The Peoples Republic of China has recently adopted a similar approach to the transfer of technology. Display items are purchased from fairs, and the Chinese elicit in the process as much technical information as possible. This technical information not only includes performance and maintenance characteristics, but extends into manufacturing techniques and the processing of basic materials.[16]

But while these many nuances in technology transfer undoubtedly occur, the description in Section II.7 is somewhat typical of technology transfer involving substantial endeavors in process technology or mass production product technology.

II.9 DEFINITION OF TECHNOLOGY TRANSFER COSTS

Having discussed the pertinent dimensions of international technology transfer, it is now possible to move toward a definition of the cost of technology transfer, a concept that has been left very vague and confused in the literature. The various actors in international technology transfer prefer to view the costs from their own perspectives.[17] The transferee may view the royalties and the technical service fees as the cost of technology transfer. The host country may view the foreign exchange costs or the political costs as the essence of technology transfer costs. The transferor on the other hand is likely to take cognizance of the opportunity costs involved when key people are taken from its organization and temporarily engaged in transfer activities. Finally, the home country may consider the erosion of its technological lead and export sales as being the key element in any calculus of transfer costs.

In order to appreciate the import of the definition that will be developed below, a distinction must be made between two basic forms in which technology can be transferred. The first form embraces physical items such as tooling, equipment and blueprints. Technology can be embodied in these objects. For example, a lathe represents embodiment of a certain amount of technical knowledge, but it is not necessary for one to know how to engineer and construct a lathe in order to operate it successfully. The second form of technology is the information that must be acquired if the physical equipment, or "hardware," is to be utilized effectively. This information relates to methods of organization and operation, quality control, and other manufacturing procedures.

Transfer of the first type of technology is a relatively straightforward operation: it involves nothing more than the physical relocation of objects.[18] Transfer of the second kind of technology is a much more complex process. It is likely to involve, among other things, consultation amongst the parties, supervision of the plant installation and design, demonstration of operating procedures by the transferor, and on the job training and learning on the part of the operatives. It is the effective conveyance of such "peripheral" support that is the crux of the process of technology transfer and it typically generates the information flow associated with it. The definition of transfer costs utilized in this study will focus on the costs of performing the activities that lead to the effective transfer of this information. It is therefore toward the cost of transfer of "unembodied"[19] knowledge that this study directs its attention. Several categories of unembodied knowledge can be identified: system-specific knowledge, firm-specific knowledge, industry-specific knowledge and basic knowledge.[20]

System-specific knowledge refers to the information possessed by a firm that has been acquired through engaging in certain projects[21] or through engaging in the manufacture of certain products. It comprises knowledge of procedures connected with a particular system or technology. This kind of information will obviously differentiate a firm from its rivals, at least to the extent that rivals have not engaged in identical activities.

Firm-specific knowledge differs from system-specific knowledge in that it cannot be attributed to any specific item the firm produces,[22] but results from the firm's overall activities. This knowledge could be organizational as well as technical.

Industry-specific knowledge refers to information common to an industry, profession or trade. This kind of information is the ticket of admission to a given industry. For instance, if consideration is given to the electrical machinery industry, then in order to enter this industry it is necessary to know how to machine parts and how to manufacture basic components such as coils and rotors. Clearly, metallurgical and electrical engineering skills are required.

The last category identified is general knowledge. This embraces information of a nonvocational nature and can be dispensed by the general education system. It would include basic skills such as arithmetic and computer programming, as well as basic mechanical skills such as the ability to perform basic engineering drafting. This kind of information will not differentiate firms from their rivals nor will it differentiate firms in one industry from firms in another.

The important distinctions between these categories relate to how the different kinds of information can be acquired and the extent to which the different kinds of information are diffused. System-specific and firm-specific information is contained only within certain enterprises, who are therefore often in a position to extract rents or royalties from the sale of this information. Industry-specific information, on the other hand, is possessed by all firms in the industry that are engaged in manufacturing a particular line of products. General information will be widely diffused amongst manufacturing enterprises in all industries. The time dimension is clearly relevant to these distinctions since information that is system-specific or firm-specific in one period may become so diffused that in the next period it can be more properly regarded as industry-specific information or general information. For example, as the number of firms that acquire a particular innovation increase, and as the relevant system-specific information becomes increasingly diffused, the knowledge concerning how to utilize an innovation will diffuse into the domain of industry-specific information. Eventually it may become general information.

Technology transfer costs are the costs of transmitting and absorbing the relevant firm-, system- and industry-specific knowledge to the extent that this is necessary for the effective transfer of the technology. The costs of performing the various activities that have to be conducted to ensure the transfer of this information will represent the cost of technology transfer.[23] Care has been taken to avoid the implication that all of the costs involved in establishing a manufacturing facility abroad can be properly regarded as technology transfer costs. Clearly, a great many skills from other industries (e.g., design engineering) will be needed for plant design, plant construction and equipment installation. However, not all of these will have to be transferred to the transferee to ensure the success of the project. The costs of transfer do not therefore include the costs of all the activities involved in establishing a plant abroad and bringing it on stream.

The definition of transfer costs presented at the conceptual level can be translated into operational measures of transfer costs by considering the nature of the activity and the costs involved. At the operational level, the subset of project costs identified as transfer costs fall into four groups. The first group is the cost of the preengineering technological exchanges. During these exchanges, the basic characteristics of the technology are revealed and the necessary theoretical insights are conveyed. Most of this information is likely to be system-specific in character.

The second group of costs included are the engineering costs associated with transferring the process design and associated process engineering[24] in the case of process innovations, or the product design and production engineering[25] in the case of product innovations. If the technology has already been commercialized, transmittal may simply involve transferring existing drawings and specifications with the minimum of modifications. However, the process of absorption may be more difficult, requiring the utilization of considerable consulting or advisory resources by the transferor to ensure that the transferee and/or the engineering contractors understand the full import of the drawings. If the technology has not been previously commercialized, or if it must undergo substantial adaptation, transfer is likely to be more complex. With process innovations, for instance, the process engineering will have to be performed before a transfer is possible. With product innovations, extensive process planning will most likely be necessary, even though the functional design and production design are preserved. Process planning requires firm-, system- and industry-specific knowledge of processes and machines. It also requires knowledge of production economics. Engineering costs not falling into any of the above categories[26] are excluded from transfer costs. The excluded engineering costs are essentially the plant or detailed engineering costs, net of supervisory and consulting costs. This residual is assumed to correspond with routine drafting[27] costs. Routine drafting is generally performed by technicians under the supervision of engineers. Accordingly, it is considered here to embody general information, and the costs are not considered to represent transfer costs.

The third group of costs are those of the R & D division (salaries and expenses) during all phases of the transfer project. These are not the R & D costs associated with developing the process or with product innovation. Rather, they are the R & D costs associated with adapting or modifying the technology. For instance, research scientists may be utilized during the transfer if new and unusual technical problems are encountered.[28] These R & D costs are generally small or nonexistent for international transfers falling into the "design transfer" category.[29] Irrespective of whether they are expended by transferor or transferee, they are included in the definition of transfer costs used in this study.

The fourth group of costs are the prestartup training costs and the excess manufacturing costs. The latter represent the learning and debugging costs incurred during the startup phase and before the plant achieves the design performance specifications. It is quite possible that no usable output will be produced during at least the initial phases of the startup. Nevertheless, labor, materials, utilities and depreciation costs will be incurred, together with the costs of the extra supervisory personnel that will inevitably be required to assist in the startup. The operating losses incurred during initial production are a close approximation to excess manufacturing costs. It is clear that, to a large extent, this fourth group of costs is a function of the factor prices and the product prices prevailing in the recipient country. However, technical efficiency is likely to be the major determinant of the excess manufacturing costs. The data to be presented will make it apparent that, for the transfers included in this study, the poststartup value of labor productivity, product quality and materials efficiency in the foreign facility was not perceived to be significantly different from the levels achieved in the domestic facility.[30] Indeed, for some projects in the sample, productivity at the termination of the startup was higher than home country productivity (see Table 1-5). For comparative purposes the transfers are accordingly considered complete.

An important consideration is the extent to which excess manufacturing costs correctly reflect technology transfer costs rather than costs of discovering and overcoming the idiosyncracies of a particular plant. One way to confront this issue is to consider the level of excess manufacturing costs when an absolutely identical plant is constructed in a location adjacent to an existing plant. Furthermore, assume that the second plant embodies the same technology as the first plant and that the labor force from the first plant performs the manufacturing startup in the second plant. The assumption is that under these circumstances excess manufacturing costs in the second plant will be zero, or very nearly so.[31] This circumstance would be identical to shutting down the first plant and then starting it up again. Some excess manufacturing costs might be incurred during the initial hours of operation if the plant embodies continuous flow process technology. However, these costs are unlikely to be of sufficient magnitude to challenge the validity of classifying excess manufacturing costs as a component of technology transfer costs.[32] Indeed, it is possible to hypothesize that the ease or difficulty of technology transfer will be closely reflected in the excess manufacturing and training costs. Excess manufacturing costs are highly sensitive to the technological and managerial competence of the transferor and the transferee. The less well the parties involved understand the technology, the higher the excess manufacturing costs. In estimates of total project costs, excess manufacturing costs are always subject to the greatest degree of uncertainty. Project managers often consider the level of realized relative to predicted excess manufacturing costs to be a good index of the technical success of a transfer project.

It seems necessary to reiterate that this definition of transfer costs relates to the costs of transferring plant by plant the ability to produce a well-defined product. It does not include the costs of transferring knowledge necessary for performing adaptations or improvements to the product or process. The dynamic dimension of technology transfer is thus omitted, although this does not rule out the consideration that such transfers may perchance occur with the transfer of manufacturing technology.

NOTES

1. See for example, R.E. Caves, "International Corporations: The Industrial Economics of Foreign Investment," *Economica* 38:1-27 (February 1971).

2. See for example, F. Arditti, "On the Separation of Production from the Developer," *Journal of Business* 41:317-28 (July 1968). Arditti points out that for transfer of the B-52F, Boeing transferred a good part of its development team to Wichita to supervise the first stages of production. From this one can infer that the transfer costs would have been quite high.

3. See, for example, E.F. Schumacher, "The Work of the Intermediate Technology Development Group in Africa," *International Labor Review* 106:75-92 (July 1972).

4. See, for example, J. Meursinge, "Practical Experience in the Transfer of Technology," *Technology and Culture* 12:469-70 (July 1971).

5. Facsimile equipment exists that can be used to instantaneously transmit messages and drawings across the Atlantic.

6. David Jones, "The 'extra costs' in Europe's Biggest Synthetic Fiber Complex at Mogilev, U.S.S.R.," *Worldwide Projects and Installations*, 7:32 (May-June 1973).

7. See J. Baranson, "Technology Transfer Through the International Firm," *American Economic Review* 60:435-40 (May 1970).

8. For a detailed exposition of these principles, see O.E. Williamson, *Markets and Hierarchies: Analysis and Antitrust Implications* (New York: Free Press, 1975).

9. One example was encountered where a Japanese firm purchased the manufacturing rights, the drawings and a sample of a piece of complex computer equipment. Even though the company had not manufactured this product before, it managed to almost completely absorb the technology with absolutely no assistance. It finally requested help in the manufacture of one component.

10. For a more comprehensive view of stages in a technology transfer project, see S. Bar-Zakay, "Technology Transfer Model," *Industrial Research and Development News* 6:1-11 (1972).

11. An example was given where negotiating an agreement with the Soviets involved 40 man-days of transferor executive time, 65 man-days of the London contractors time and 3,000 man-days of the Japanese contractors time.

12. These technologies are differentiated according to whether the underlying innovations can be regarded as process or product. A process innovation is distinguished from a product innovation in that whereas the latter results in a new product, the former results in an improved method or in production of an existing product. Very often a product innovation will involve process innovation, so that the distinctions are not always very clear.

13. This term is used according to the definition in Section I.4.

14. See G.R. Hall and R.D. Johnson, "Transfers of United States Aerospace Technology to Japan," in R. Vernon, ed., *The Technology Factor in International Trade* (New York: National Bureau of Economic Research, 1970),

especially p. 333, for a particular example. The first 29 Japanese engines were supplied from the U.S. as partly assembled knockdowns, but imports declined dramatically thereafter.

15. See W.O. Henderson, *Britain and Industrial Europe 1750-1870* (Leicester, England: Leicester University Press, 1972).

16. See J. Baranson, "Technical Improvement in Developing Countries," *Finance and Development* 11:2-5 (June 1974).

17. For two contrasting approaches, see R. Hal Mason, "The Multinational Firm and the Cost of Technology to Developing Countries," *California Management Review* 15:5-13 (Summer 1973); and R. Gillette, "Latin America: Is Imported Technology Too Expensive?" *Science* 181:41-44 (July 1973).

18. Hall and Johnson concur that the process of technology transfer "is simpler if knowledge is embodied in purely physical items" (p. 306).

19. "Unembodied" knowledge is the term used here to denote knowledge not embodied in capital goods, blueprints and technical specifications, etc.

20. This terminology is similar but not identical to that used by Hall and Johnson. (Note that knowledge, skills and information are used more or less synonymously in this study.)

21. For example, participation in a particular R & D project will lead to the creation of system-specific knowledge that will distinguish a firm from its rivals, particularly if the R & D project results in the production of a significant innovation.

22. Knowledge of the business and technical environment in foreign countries falls into this category.

23. All the relevant costs are included irrespective of which entity initially or eventually incurs them.

24. Recall from Section II.5 that process engineering for continuous flow technology involves the compilation of flow diagrams, heat balances and control instrumentation, etc. It can be distinguished from detailed engineering, which involves the translation and elaboration of the process engineering into a manufacturing facility.

25. Recall from Section II.5 that production engineering for a specified item can be divided into two phases:

(a) Production design: This is the modification of the functional design in order to reduce manufacturing costs. (Functional product design is the design of a product to fulfill certain specifications and requirements.)

(b) Process planning: Given the design, process planning for manufacture must be carried out to specify, in careful detail, the processes required and their sequence. The production design first sets the minimum possible cost that can be achieved through the specification of materials, tolerances, basic configurations, methods of joining parts, etc. Process planning then attempts to achieve that minimum through the specification of processes and their sequence to meet the exacting requirements of the design specifications. The accepted end point for production design is manifested by the drawing release, which summarizes the exact specifications of what is to be made. Process planning takes over from this point and develops the broad plan of manufacture for the part or product. A distinction can also be drawn between process planning blends with the layout of physical facilities. Some process planning will take place during the layout phases of the design of a production system. Process plans can be regarded as inputs to the development of a layout. For further elaboration of these concepts, see for example, *McGraw-Hill Encyclopedia of Science and Technology* (New York: McGraw-Hill, 1960), vol. 10, pp. 639-44.

26. The above categories referred to are (a) process of design engineering costs and related consultation, (b) costs of engineering supervision and consultation (salaries plus travel and living) for the plant or detailed engineering, and (c) production engineering expenses for product innovations).

27. For further discussion of the nature of drafting activities, see *McGraw-Hill Encyclopedia of Science and Technology*, vol. 4, p. 271.

28. Referring to process technologies, it is possible that differences in feedstocks at home and abroad may create problems that only research scientists can effectively handle. Similarly, changes in atmospheric conditions or water supply could have unexpected consequences for some highly complex processes.

29. "Design transfer" is used according to the definition in Section I.4.

30. This is not surprising, since, for a sample of U.S. multinational companies, Mordechai Kreinin found that labor time per unit of output in U.S. plants was only at most 20-25 percent lower than for the European plants. See his "Comparative Labor Effectiveness and the Leontief Scarce-Factor Paradox," *American Economic Review* 55:131-40 (March 1965).

31. The correctness of this assumption was corroborated by a subsample of project managers subsequently questioned about this matter.

32. For the projects in the sample the average duration of the manufacturing startup was 8.2 months.

Chapter Three

The Level and Determinants
of the Cost of International
Technology Transfer:
Data and Hypotheses

III.1 INTRODUCTION

This chapter presents descriptive statistics on the level of transfer cost for a sample of 26 transfers.[1] It also contains a detailed elaboration of the factors considered to be important determinants of technology transfer costs. With respect to this, considerable attention is given to the development of hypotheses regarded as testable in the light of available data. Three groups of variables will be presented: variables relating to characteristics of the technology, variables relating to characteristics of the transferee and variables relating to the host country infrastructure.

III.2 DESCRIPTIVE STATISTICS ON THE RESOURCE
COSTS OF TECHNOLOGY TRANSFER

Employing the definition outlined in Section II.9, the transfer costs for each of the projects in the sample were calculated. The results of these calculations are presented in the table below. Transfer costs are given first in their absolute dollar values. These are then normalized by dividing through by total project costs.[2] The total project costs are the costs of Stages A, B, C and D as defined in Section II.7.

Wherever a clear separation of excess manufacturing and training costs could be made this was noted and summary statistics on these findings are presented in Table 3-3.

The sample data in Table 3-1 indicate that the resource costs of horizontal transfers to locations abroad are by no means trivial. For

Table 3-1.   Sample Data on Transfer Costs (The Resource Costs of Transfer: Absolute Dollar Amounts and Dollar Amounts Expressed as a Percentage of Total Project Costs)

Chemicals and Petroleum Refining		Machinery	
Transfer Costs: Dollar Amount (thousands)	Transfer Costs: Dollar Amount Total Project Cost	Transfer Costs: Dollar Amount (thousands)	Transfer Costs: Dollar Amount Total Project Cost
49.86	18.40	198.75	26.50
185.36	8.00	360.00	32.00
683.20	11.20	1,006.57	38.20
137.19	17.06	5,850.00	45.00
449.45	8.90	555.90	10.90
362.04	7.37	1,530.36	42.51
643.41	6.64	33.63	59.00
75.46	10.75	968.40	24.21
780.00	13.00	270.00	45.00
2,142.68	6.80		
161.59	2.25		
586.35	7.48		
877.82	7.30		
66.80	4.00		
2,850.00	19.00		
7,425.00	22.00		
3,341.22	4.78		

the sample as a whole, transfer costs are on average 19.16 percent of total project costs. Although transfer costs are clearly nontrivial, some attempt must be made to put them in perspective, since they can only be judged as "high" or "low" according to some reference level. It would, for instance, be of some interest to know how large these costs are compared to the costs of performing other types of innovative activity. Unfortunately, data are not available to compare the relative costs of these essentially "horizontal" transfers with the costs of "vertical" technology transfers across the various interfaces encountered in the innovation process. While not addressing themselves exactly to this question, Mansfield et al.[3] have identified stages in the innovation process and presented costs for a small sample of innovations. While transfer costs are not separated from the other costs in the innovative process, the sample data is of interest since stage four (tooling and manufacturing facilities) in the Mansfield study seems to correspond exactly with Stage C as defined in the present study. In the Mansfield study, the total front end costs—

Table 3-2. Summary Statistics (transfer costs expressed as a percentage of total project cost)

	Chemicals and Petroleum Refining	Machinery	Total Sample
minimum	2.25	10.90	2.25
maximum	22.00	59.00	59.00
mean	10.28	35.92	19.16
standard deviation	5.73	14.20	15.50
sample size	17	9	26

Table 3-3. Excess Manufacturing and Training Costs as a Percentage of Total Transfer Costs: Summary Statistics

	Chemicals and Petroleum Refining	Machinery	Total Sample
mean	40.79	63.25	48.33
maximum	75	93	93
minimum	3	20	3
sample size	14	4	18

represented by the sum of stages one through three—are 1.31 times the tooling and plant costs. In this study, the strictly transfer costs are 0.30 times the tooling and plant costs. Hence, although many front end costs are avoided in technology transfer, horizontal transfers involve significant costs. These seem to be high even compared to the costs of knowledge discovery and transfer in the innovation process. Clearly, there seems little room for the notion that transfer costs are zero, or very nearly so.

Nevertheless, there is considerable variation in the sample data, and it is clear that transfer costs expressed as a percentage of total project costs are lower in the chemical and petroleum refining subsample than in the machinery subsample. This indicates that for the former subsample transfer costs are a relatively less significant factor in the calculus of total project costs. Further, the findings summarized in Table 3-3 indicate that about half of the transfer costs are excess manufacturing and training costs incurred as the labor force is gaining familiarity with the technology. These costs are especially high in the machinery subsample, where learning curves are probably shallower than in the chemicals and petroleum refining subsample. Therefore, in some cases a good deal of the resources employed in technology transfer are expended on in-plant learning. The utilization of home country managers and engineers and attendant transmittal costs, although critical to the success of the transfer, do not always account for the largest element of the dollar value of the resources employed in technology transfer.[4]

While variation in the relative levels of various components of the technology transfer costs is itself a topic of some interest, the primary goal of the rest of this chapter is to discuss hypotheses developed to explain the level of total transfer costs, normalized for project size. The next section will provide an introduction to some of the relevant considerations.

III.3 DETERMINANTS OF COST OF INTERNATIONAL TECHNOLOGY TRANSFER: INTRODUCTORY COMMENTS:

Technology transfer costs are the costs of transmitting and absorbing the relevant firm-, system-, and industry-specific knowledge. (An operational definition of transfer costs was presented in Section II.9.) The number of factors influencing transfer costs is clearly quite enormous. However, some factors are likely to have a more pervasive influence than others. This section introduces hypotheses that represent attempts to highlight factors considered to have an important bearing on the cost of international technology transfer. The next four sections will present an elaboration and restructuring of some of these hypotheses in a manner conducive to statistical testing. Chapter Four presents the results of these statistical tests. Since not all of the propositions advanced in this section undergo statistical testing, they should be given close scrutiny.

In order to systematize the presentation, the factors hypothesized to affect transfer costs are classified into four groups. The first relates to characteristics of the transferor, the second to characteristics of the transferee, the third to characteristics of the technology and the fourth to characteristics of the host country economic infrastructure.

Consider first the characteristics of the transferor. Experience with international operations and with technology transfer may well be a prerequisite for success in the transfer of complex manufacturing systems.[5] Many corporations actively engaged in technology transfer have experience built up over many years. A foreign market is generally first supplied by export, and this activity gives the potential transferor a feel for the business environment abroad. Eventually manufacturing facilities may be located abroad and most companies count as important the knowledge they have gained through prior market contact. Experience with tastes, skills, attitudes and knowledge of the infrastructure of the host country will become part of the knowledge possessed by the transferor. Generally, successful foreign operations depend on an enlightened approach to foreign skills and capabilities. Several respondents in this study pointed out that at first they seriously underestimated the ability and capacity for learning of the foreign labor force, and in some cases this led to an overly paternalistic approach and a misallocation of resources. It was also felt that a corporation must be sensitive to and realistic about the differences—political, social and economic—between the foreign and the home environment. These considerations are likely to be particularly relevant to the transfer of technology within the various branches of the multinational corporation, for in these cases the transferor typically exercises tighter control. The orientation of senior executives has been classified as ethnocentric, polycentric and geocentric[6] according to the degree to which a corporation maintains a transideological view of its operations. For instance, the geocentric model applies where senior executives do not assume the inherent superiority of the home office and seek to find the best man, irrespective of nationality, to solve the company's problems, including problems relating to technology transfer. On the other hand, when technology is transferred to independent enterprises in which the transferor has no equity, there is more scope for protesting and rejecting practices that are regarded as incorrect or undesirable. In these cases the ideological and behavioral characteristics of the transferor are less important. Generally, the geocentric view seems to be a function of international experience, and enterprises possessing this orientation attached importance to it in evaluating the success of their technology transfer activities.

The second group of factors to be discussed relate to the characteristics of the technology. A critical factor will be the extent to which the technology is understood by the transferor,[7] and, as will be seen in the next section, the number of manufacturing startups that the transferor has already conducted with a specific technology is used as an index of this. Corporations engaged in technology transfer ventures not grounded on their own technology have encountered massive transfer problems and costs.[8] On the other hand, transfers that have taken place previously are often regarded, *ceteris paribus*, as the least costly to perform.

Another characteristic of the technology likely to be important is the extent to which the transfer is of a complete manufacturing system or a part of a manufacturing system: e.g., assembly and testing operations only. Generally, it would seem that, in the machinery category, for instance, the transfer of a total manufacturing system might involve relatively large transfer costs compared to the costs of transferring just the assembly activities. In order to conduct integrated production abroad, a knowledge of the whole system might need to be transferred. In comparison, systems problems can generally be solved at headquarters if just an assembly operation is transferred. Further, later stages of the production process are likely to involve activities that are less sophisticated and less demanding of skills than are earlier phases.

Other characteristics of the technology hypothesized to influence transfer costs are its age and the extent of diffusion. The age of an innovation will determine the stability of the engineering designs and the knowledge of the manufacturing procedure. The hypothesized effect of these considerations on transfer cost is elaborated in the next section. Furthermore, the greater the extent to which the innovation and associated manufacturing skills have been diffused, the lower the costs of technology transfer, the hypothesis being that the degree of diffusion is likely to be an index of the extent to which the relevant skills are available locally and do not need therefore to be imported or developed.

The third group of factors to be discussed relate to the characteristics of the transferee. First of all, it seems clear that the technical and managerial competence of the transferee will be an important determinant of the ease with which technology can be absorbed. In particular, the number and quality of manufacturing engineers are likely to be a key determinant of the transfer costs, since it is the manufacturing engineers who are the key actors in horizontal technology transfer, acting as the conduits through which the technology is filtered into the enterprise. Research and development personnel play a relatively insignificant role unless the technology has not been previously commercialized, in which case research and development personnel could play a significant consultative role. Research and development capability is not likely to be important unless the product is extremely complex and unusual problems are encountered. Research and development scientists generally understand the product and the science sufficiently well to grapple successfully with new and unique circumstances. A process or production engineer may not have the necessary background to handle these problems without assistance. The extent to which manufacturing and technical skills have been developed in the transferee is likely in turn to be a function of many factors, such as the amount of manufacturing experience, and perhaps the size of the transferee. Second, the nature of the organizational linkage between transferor and transferee ought to be examined for possible impact on transfer cost.

The last group of factors to be discussed relate to the characteristics of the host country economic infrastructure. Characteristics of the sociocultural infrastructure exert an important influence on the success of technology transfer. Attitudinal factors, for instance, will determine the willingness of society to accept imported technology and the associated sociocultural changes. While not minimizing the importance of these considerations, the focus of this study is more on the economic and technical dimensions of technology transfer. Thus, no attention is given to the network of information flows that leads to the eventual coupling of transferor and transferee.[9] Rather, attention is focused on the transfer of design capacity and the attendant technical information. A transfer successful in this respect could yet fail if the sale of the final product depends on local acceptance and if this is not forthcoming. Accordingly, the more relevant dimensions of the host country infrastructure are the availability of skills, component supplies and utilities. However, it should be noted that the level of economic development of the host country will reflect to some extent the general characteristics of host country firms. Clearly some firms will be significantly advanced beyond the average level of development, but, in general, the characteristics of the infrastructure will be subsumed under the characteristics of host country firms. Furthermore, it is these firms that are likely to be selected if a foreign firm is seeking a joint venture partner or a licensee. In addition, the dual economy[10] characteristic of less developed countries would in and of itself suggest that some transfers to the modern sector of less developed countries might proceed quite smoothly and at relatively moderate transfer costs. But even if transfers at the margin proceed in this manner, it would not be correct to infer that all conceivable transfers would share these characteristics.

The remaining sections in this chapter are an attempt to present these sets of hypotheses in a manner amenable to statistical testing. The list of propositions will be narrowed by eliminating the ones that are more difficult to test with the available data. Variables will be defined that purport to quantify the various considerations outlined above. Wherever possible, the hypotheses and variables will be juxtaposed and compared.

III.4 CHARACTERISTICS OF THE TECHNOLOGY

The first variable to be considered in detail is the number of previous manufacturing startups[11] of a specific technology by the transferor.

An increase in the number of manufacturing startups is likely to lower transfer costs for several reasons. First, startups enhance the manufacturer's fundamental understanding of the technology. Second, certain elements of the engineering need only be duplicated for startups subsequent to the first. Third, operator training can often be facilitated by the existence of an already established facility that can be used for training a new group of operators. Each of these considerations will now be considered separately.

The number of manufacturing startups that a transferor has conducted for a given technology is an important index of how well the firm understands the technology and, hence, of how capable the firm is likely to be at transferring the technology associated with a given innovation. With each startup, additional knowledge about the technology is acquired. No two startups are identical, and with each startup the firm has the opportunity of observing the effect of different operating parameters and differences in equipment design. Each startup can be regarded as a new experiment that yields new information and new experience. Adaptation will also be facilitated the more fully the technology is understood.

Furthermore, the first startup represents the first commercialization of the technology. This will result in the creation of a set of basic engineering drawings and specifications. Duplication of these will involve a very small cost compared to the initial costs of constructing them.

Besides these engineering type economies there are also significant advantages that can accrue from the expanded opportunities for prestartup training of the labor force. More complete prestartup training can markedly lower excess manufacturing costs. The extent to which these savings can be realized will depend on the geographical proximity of a proposed startup to any previous startup site for the technology. Clearly, if a similar plant exists nearby, then experienced operators can be used to assist the startup in the new plant and untrained operators can be brought into the existing plant for training. Excess manufacturing costs are generally a large element of total transfer costs, so the potential savings can be quite large. However, it is seldom that subsequent startups occur under such idealized conditions. They are generally geographically separate from earlier ones and the technology may be altered to take account of recent improvements and the special circumstances surrounding each application. If improvements are continually being effected in the technology, there will be little incentive to duplicate an already existing facility. For instance, in some industries the optimum economic size is increasing so rapidly that the last project may be uneconomically small at the time an international transfer is contemplated. Scale-up may be required. Conversely, there may be some industries where scale-down is needed because of the small size of the foreign market to which a transfer is contemplated. Such exercises in scale alteration may diminish the savings that would otherwise arise from repeating a startup. Even if for these reasons each additional startup subsequent to the first does not result in savings, it is still likely that the very first startup will involve substantially higher costs than subsequent startups. The reason is that if the technology has never been utilized in a plant of commercial size, then the costs of going from development prototypes or pilot plants to commercial production can be quite high, because of high excess manufacturing costs and because the production or process engineering drawings must first be created, and communication between the development and production groups will be necessary. Even when the first startup proceeds proximate to the development site, the problems of communication and interaction between development and manufacturing can be considerable. If geographical, cultural and economic barriers are superimposed across the transfer interface, the problems of transferring technology will be compounded.

The second variable to be considered is the age of the technology. The age of the technology is defined here as the number of years since the beginning of the first commercial application of the technology[12] anywhere in the world, and the end[13] of the technology transfer program. The beginning of the first commercial implementation will be different from the end of the development phase by the extent to which there is overlap with the manufacturing startup phase.

The age of an innovation will determine the stability of the engineering designs and the knowledge of the manufacturing procedure. The older the innovation, *ceteris paribus*, then the greater have been the opportunities for interaction between the development groups and the manufacturing or operating groups. Problems stand a better chance of being ironed out, and the drawings are likely to be more secure. Further, technology is not embodied in drawings alone; a great deal of it is noncodified information or "art." This kind of knowledge is embodied in supervisors, engineers and operators. As the age of the innovation increases, more individuals become acquainted with this noncodified information and hence are potentially available to assist in the transfer. Operations in the transferor will be less sensitive to withdrawal of key people and so the transfer is likely to proceed more smoothly and at lower cost. There will, however, be some point at which greater age begins to increase the cost of transfer. When the length of stay of corporate personnel begins to be outstripped by the age of the technology, then the noncodified dimensions of design knowledge may be lost to the firm and hence will no longer be available at the time of a transfer. Further, the drawings associated with technology that is very old may suffer from so many small alterations that the essence of the technology may become obscure. In the limit, the firm could terminate its utilization of this technology and the noncodified information associated with it could be lost forever as the innovation becomes historic. However, most of the technology transfer projects in the sample involve relatively recent innovations, and it may therefore be necessary to focus attention only on that range of the function where there is an inverse relationship between the age of the technology and the cost of its transfer.

It is necessary to distinguish the cost reductions resulting from additional startups from the cost reductions resulting from greater age of the technology. The distinction may depend to some extent on the type of technology discussed. For instance, it is plausible that, at least for continuous flow technologies, additional applications of an innovation in entirely new plants will allow experimentation not only with scale but also with basic parameters of the design. This will generate new information about the technology. On the other hand, greater age, holding the number of applications or startups constant, generally only permits experimentation with some of the operating parameters, the plant design remaining fixed throughout. Both types of experimentation generate information that is very useful if transfer is to be attempted with or without adaptation.

The third variable to be considered is the number of firms utilizing similar and competitive technology. The number of firms throughout the world utilizing an innovation will be an indication of the degree to which the innovation and the associated manufacturing technology is diffused throughout the industry at the time the transfer program is commenced. The greater the number of firms with similar and competitive technology, then the greater the likelihood that firm-specific and system-specific technology is moving into the domain of industry-specific and basic technology.[14] Technology transfer is facilitated to the extent that it is dependent on the latter categories rather than on system- and firm-specific technology. This is because less information will have to be imported and mastered. Therefore, it seems reasonable to hypothesize that transfer costs will be lower the greater the number of firms commercially utilizing the technology.[15] Clearly, this variable is not a very precise measure of the degree of diffusion, since some industries are more concentrated than others. However, it is likely to be a sufficiently good approximation where the variable takes small values and amongst industries that are relatively homogeneous.

III.5 THE TECHNOLOGY VARIABLES: A SYNTHESIS

When examined singularly, the technology variables define the technology to only a limited extent. However, they begin to take on extra meaning when viewed together. *Ceteris paribus*, the most difficult and hence costly technology to transfer is characterized by very few previous manufacturing startups, very few other firms with a competitive technology and very short duration since first manufacturing startup.

Technology having such characteristics will be termed "leading edge" technology. It is likely to be in a state of flux: the engineering drawings will be constantly changing, thus frustrating a transfer. Manufacturing problems will not be ironed out, and so the excess manufacturing costs will be higher than otherwise. In comparison, state of the art technology will, *ceteris paribus*, be relatively simple to transfer; the drawings are more likely to be finalized, and although some modifications may be necessary, the fundamentals of the process will be well understood.

III.6 TRANSFEREE CHARACTERISTICS

The first variable to be considered is the number of years of manufacturing experience possessed by the transferee. Experience is defined as the number of years of manufacturing experience in a given four digit ISIC industry classification at the time startup commenced.[16] This variable is taken to be an index of the extent to which managers, engineers and operatives have command over the general manufacturing skills of an industry. A firm skilled in the manufacture of some group of products is likely to have less difficulty absorbing a new innovation in that industry group than is the firm that has had no previous experience manufacturing products in a particular industry group.

The criterion used to define the relevant industry group is the International Standard Industrial Classification (ISIC). One of the major classificatory considerations underlying the ISIC is the technology and the organization of production.[17] Producing units are grouped according to degrees of similarity in cost structures, the relative magnitudes of fixed capital and labor employed, and relative productivity and scale of operation. For the purpose in hand, the ISIC would therefore seem to be an appropriate classification.

The second variable to be considered is the size of the transferee. The value of total annual sales at the beginning of the transfer is used as an index of firm size. If there have been no previous sales, then initial sales after startup is taken as an index of size. Larger firms might be expected to have lower transfer costs, since larger firms are generally characterized by greater specialization and, hence, there is likely to be a larger number of R & D, engineering and managerial personnel who can be called on if needed during the transfer.[18] A smaller firm might have to hire these consultants, or to try and do without. If consultants have to be hired, this will impose transactions costs that would be absent if resources were internally available.

The third variable to be considered is the research and development expenditures to sales ratio of the transferee at the beginning of transfer. In some circumstances, the presence of research and development capability can affect the cost of technology transfer. Sometimes a transfer can encounter unusual technical problems that production or process engineers do not have the necessary theoretical insight to handle. Such problems might arise, for instance, during the transfer of leading edge technology. Research and development personnel have the ability to handle whatever new and unique problems may be encountered.[19]

The fourth and fifth variables relate to the organizational linkage established between the transferor and transferee. It is argued here and in Sections II.8 and V.4 that transfer mode has some bearing on total project cost. Under circumstances of uncertainty and bounded rationality[20] the internal transfer of technology might economize on transactions costs. Where uncertainties are most prevalent, all activities of the project—including transfer activities—are likely to proceed at lower cost if the project is internalized. That is, transfers to affiliates are hypothesized to proceed at lower costs, *ceteris paribus*, than are transfers to nonaffiliates. Furthermore, transfers to government enterprises in centrally planned economies involve extra costs because of the procedural differences[21] involved and the extra documentation that is generally required.

III.7 ECONOMIC INFRASTRUCTURE OF THE HOST COUNTRY

The economic and technical dimensions of the host country infrastructure embrace factors such as the skills and educational level of the labor force, the availability of utilities and the capabilities of domestic suppliers. The level of skills will determine the amount and type of training and on the job learning required, the availability of utilities will influence the investments that have to be made before the actual transfer begins, and the capabilities of domestic suppliers will determine which inputs are purchased locally and which are imported. In many cases a venture can bypass problems of local supply by importing components, but if this option is not available or not taken, then the capabilities of suppliers could have a large impact on the costs of transfer.[2 2]

The level of GNP per capita will be used as an index of the level of economic development of the host country. Various aggregate studies point to strong cross-sectional correlations between GNP per capita and indices of educational levels, development of utilities, wage rates, etc. While this variable has a large number of deficiencies as a measure of the development of the economic infrastructure, it is a convenient summary index and may be sufficiently good as a first approximation.

NOTES

1. Transfer costs could not be obtained for three of the transfers included in the sample.

2. Total project costs are measured according to the inside boundary limits definition. Costs incurred outside the boundary limits—the installation of some utilities, for example—are thereby excluded.

3. E. Mansfield et al., *Research and Innovation in the Modern Corporation* (New York: W.W. Norton, 1971), ch. 6.

4. G.R. Hall and R.E. Johnson, "Transfers of United States Aerospace Technology to Japan," in R. Vernon, ed., *The Technology Factor in International Trade* (New York: National Bureau of Economic Research, 1970), p. 340, also indicate that "technical assistance" costs were relatively low for the transfer of F104-J technology.

5. Because the relevant data was not collected, hypotheses relating to the firms' overall experience with international operations and technology transfer were not tested. However, an attempt to measure the firms' experience in transferring a particular innovation is contained in the "number of manufacturing startups variable" defined below.

6. See H.V. Perlmutter, "Social Architectural Problems of the Multinational Firm," *Quarterly Journal of AIESEC International* 3 (August 1967).

7. This factor could be classified as a characteristic of the transferor.

8. For example, a U.S. oil company decided to establish a huge fertilizer project in a less developed country. The project was based on another company's process. The resultant cost overruns were an embarrassment to it for several years.

9. For a wide ranging discussion of some of these issues, see W. Gruber and D. Marquis, eds., *Factors in the Transfer of Technology* (Cambridge: M.I.T. Press, 1969).

10. See, for example, W.A. Lewis, "Economic Development with Unlimited Supplies of Labor," *The Manchester School* 22:139-91 (May 1954).

11. The number of manufacturing startups by the transferor will be identical to the number of plants it has built to utilize the technology if a new plant is built for each application.

12. If there is more than one key innovation embodied in the technology then the date of commercial implementation of the most recent key innovation is the reference date (see Appendix B).

13. Age is defined up to the end of the transfer program since any knowledge about the technology acquired up to this point is potentially useful for the transfer. For the first startups, age will be the length of the transfer minus the development overlap.

14. These terms were defined in Section I.5 of this study.

15. There will be a problem of simultaneous equation bias if the "number of firms" with similar and competitive technology is a function of transfer cost. This will be compounded by an identification problem if the other arguments entering the transfer cost function are the same as those entering the number of firms function, but on a priori grounds this seems unlikely.

16. Prestartup training is treated as manufacturing experience, even if it is not acquired on site. Hence, even a completely new organization will be endowed with some manufacturing experience so long as there has been some prestartup training.

17. See United Nations, *International Standard Industrial Classification of all Economic Activity*, United Nations Statistical Papers, series M, no. 4 (New York, 1968).

18. Furthermore, since larger firms may also be older firms, they are likely to possess more operating experience than smaller firms, but not necessarily in the relevant product or process areas.

19. On the other hand, a research and development capability could be detrimental to a transfer if it fosters a "not invented here" syndrome. While research and development can generate enthusiasm for new ideas, this enthusiasm can become deleterious if it is restricted to only those ideas that are generated internally.

20. See O.E. Williamson, *Markets and Hierarchies: Analysis and Antitrust Implications* (New York: Free Press, 1975).

21. Formal approvals are generally required for all actions, and guarantees may be demanded for all phases of the project.

22. See, for example, J. Baranson, *Manufacturing Problems in India: The Cummins Diesel Experience* (Syracuse, N.Y.: Syracuse University Press, 1967).

※ *Chapter Four*

Determinants of the Cost of International Technology Transfer: Tests and Results

IV.1 INTRODUCTION

Two different kinds of cost data have been collected in order that statistical testing of the hypotheses can proceed.

The first contains the various elements of the costs incurred in implementing a sample of projects around the world. This data will serve as the basis for a regression analysis that seeks to identify the variables that have the strongest impact on the technology transfer costs. The second contains estimates provided by executives on how these costs would vary under certain hypothetical but quite ordinary circumstances. This kind of data has the advantage that other variables have been held constant. Because missing variables are held constant by this procedure, there is a greater chance that variables with quite small effects can be identified. Moreover, it is possible that a more precise form of the function can be fitted. An added advantage of collecting both kinds of data is that a check for internal consistency is available. Given the small size of the sample, and the fact that no comparable research has been done using the variables employed in this study, it will be comforting if two separate kinds of analysis produce similar results. One of the best tests of any hypothesis is to look for the convergence of two independent lines of evidence.

IV.2 THE MODEL

The basic model to be tested is

57

$$C_i = f(U_i, G_i, E_i, R_i, S_i, N_i, O_{1i}, O_{2i}, P_i, Z_i)$$ (4.1)

C_i is the transfer cost divided by the total project cost for the ith transfer. U_i is the number of previous manufacturing startups that the technology of the ith transfer has undergone by the transferring firm. G_i is the age of this technology in years. E_i is the number of years of manufacturing experience that the recipient (i.e., the trans-feree) of the ith transfer has accumulated. R_i is the ratio of research and development to value of sales for the recipient of the ith trans-fer. N_i is the number of firms identified as possessing a technology that is "similar and competitive" to the technology underlying the ith transfer. O_{1i} is a variable that takes the value of 1 if the recipient of the ith transfer is an affiliate of the transferor, and takes the value of zero otherwise. O_{2i} is a variable that takes the value of 1 if the recipient of the ith transfer is a government-controlled enterprise, and takes the value zero otherwise. P_i is the level of GNP per capita of the host country. Z_i is the random error term for the ith transfer.

The testing of this model will proceed in two phases. First, cross-section data on actually implemented projects is utilized in a linear version of the model employing ordinary least squares proce-dures. Second, estimated cost data on the projects is pooled and employed to test a more specific nonlinear version of the model. A third phase of the statistical testing seeks to employ a simple linear model to explain differences in the estimated costs of domestic and international transfers.

IV.3 STATISTICAL TESTS: PHASE I

Consider the dependent variable. It has been necessary to find some way of normalizing transfer costs to take account of the fact that the projects within the sample vary enormously in size. The procedure adopted was to present the transfer cost as a percentage of total project costs, as defined in Section II.7. Within an industry this would seem to provide an appropriate normalization. In chemicals, for instance, the capital investment is very large and there are limited capital-labor substitution possibilities. The normalization procedure would therefore seem to be acceptable. Scale factors can be taken into account by including the size of the capital investment as an independent variable in the regression analysis. For transfers in the machinery category where the technology offers greater opportuni-ties for capital-labor substitution, the procedure may be less trust-worthy. Because of considerations such as these, a certain amount of "noise" can be expected in the models. Further, a certain amount of the interindustry differences may be accounted for by inadequacies in the normalization procedure.

The model to be tested in Phase I is:

$$C_i = \alpha_0 + \alpha_1 U_i + \alpha_2 G_i + \alpha_3 E_i + \alpha_4 R_i + \alpha_5 S_i$$

$$+ \alpha_6 N_i + \alpha_7 O_{1i} + \alpha_8 O_{2i} + \alpha_9 P_i + Z_i \qquad (4.2)$$

In the first instance, the model was estimated for the total sample using a dummy variable to pool the two subsamples. This did not produce statistically significant results for any of the independent variables except the interindustry dummy. A disaggregation of the data into the two subsamples eased the problem and at the same time suggested not only that the costs of transfer are determined by a different subset of variables in the different industries, but also that the magnitude of the impact of identified variables is different for the two subsamples.[1] The results are presented in Table 4-1.[2] Variables whose coefficients are not significant at the 0.05 level are not included in Equation 4.1. They were sequentially dropped. Equation 4.2 contains a variable that approached significance. Application of a forward stepwise procedure did not suggest that any other combinations of the variable would improve the equations.

Consider the implication of these results for the model. In the chemical and petroleum refining subsample, the dummy variable representing the number of previous manufacturing startups is significant. The variable takes the value of 1 if the observation represents the first startup (i.e., first commercialization), and the value zero otherwise. Clearly, then, the resource costs of transfer in the sample are higher if the international transfer is of a technology that has not been previously commercialized and is therefore untried in a fully fledged manufacturing operation. Apparently, once the technology has been commercialized, extra startups do not produce a statistically significant lowering of transfer costs in the chemical industry subsample. The number of firms variable is also significant in this subsample indicating that the extent to which the technology is diffused in the industry is also an important determinant of the transfer costs.[3] The years of manufacturing experience in a given four digit industry was the only other variable that proved significant on a one tail test at the 0.06 significance level. One other variable approached significance: sales value of the transferee. However, it is not possible to be more than 85 percent sure that the sign is correct or that the coefficient is indeed different from zero. G_i, O_{2i}, O_{1i}, P_i, R_i were not significant in any of the regression equations utilizing the chemical and petroleum refining data.

Table 4-1.　Regression of Coefficients and t Statistics in Regression Equations to Explain C (the cost of transfer)

Independent variable	Chemicals and Petroleum Refining		Machinery	
	Equation 1	Equation 2	Equation 1	Equation 2
Constant	12.79	13.42	66.67	65.98
	(6.82)	(6.98)	(8.27)	(6.60)
Zero startup dummy variable*	6.73	6.11	–	1.62
	(1.92)	(1.75)		(0.15)
Number of firms variable	–0.37	–0.39	–1.29	–1.26
	(–2.06)	(–2.22)	(–2.28)	(–1.95)
Age of technology variable (years)	–	–	–2.43	–2.35
			(–3.53)	(–2.51)
Experience of transferee variable (years in Four digit ISIC)	–0.09	–0.08	–0.84	–0.85
	(–1.66)	(–1.42)	(–3.37)	(–2.95)
Size of transferee variable (thousands of dollars of sales)	–	–0.0009	–	–
		(–1.18)		
Number of observations	17	17	9	9
R^2	0.56	0.61	0.78	0.78
F	5.66	4.73	6.00	3.22
Significance level of F	0.01	0.02	0.04	0.12

*The number of previous manufacturing startups was significant in Phase I only when it was included as a dummy variable taking the value 1 if there had been no previous manufacturing startups of this technology by the transferring firm, and zero otherwise.

Consider the machinery subsample. The equation that yielded the best fit and contained significant variables is similar to the previous equations except that the age of the technology variable is significant, whereas the dummy for zero startups is not. Apparently the age of the technology rather than the number of startups is the governing consideration. This admits of an explanation in line with the hypothesis advanced earlier. Once manufacturing has commenced, there exists more latitude for manufacturing experimentation with machinery type technologies than with continuous flow technologies, where the fixed investment is often huge and design changes are accordingly expensive. That is, in the former category, there is some freedom to adjust the basic parameters of the technology. In addition to the number of startups variable, the size variable, the R & D to sales variable and the other hypothesized variables did not approach acceptable significance in any of the equations estimated for the machinery category. However, it is interesting to note that the coefficient of the experience variable is considerably larger in the machinery category than in the chemicals and petroleum refining category. This could be a reflection of the greater learning economies and resultant greater excess manufacturing costs. In semiconductors and aircraft, for instance, learning economies have always been substantial, while in a typical chemical plant learning economies exist but they are not as important.[4]

IV.4 STATISTICAL TESTS: PHASE II

It was pointed out in the previous section that one of the difficulties presented by the testing of a model such as (4.2) is that there is little variation in some of the exogenous variables. This lack of variation, coupled with the problem of omitted variables, implies difficulties with bias and identification.

For the projects in the sample, a procedure was devised to hold the missing variables constant and to generate large variation in the exogenous variables. Respondents were asked to estimate how the total transfer costs would vary for each case if one particular exogenous variable happened to take a different value, assuming all other variables to be constant. The responses were taken into account only if such an exercise generated circumstances within the bounds of an executive's experience.[5] Given these limitations, the change specified was quite large, in order to provide a robust sample. Generally, the actual value of a selected variable was hypothesized first to half, and then to double.[6] The estimated impact on total transfer costs was noted. This exercise was performed for the K independent variables. The independent variables are given as follows: (1) the number of startups that the technology has undergone; (2) the age of the technology; (3) the number of years of previous manufacturing experience possessed by the transferee in a given four digit industry; (4) the research and development expenditures to sales ratio of the transferee; (5) the size (measured by sales value) of the transferee. For each of these variables[7] this exercise with a given executive generated at most three observations on transfer costs for each project. Pooling all of the available observations produces enough observations for ordinary least squares regression analysis.

It is convenient to begin the estimation procedure by assuming that the shape of the cost functions can be represented by the following relatively simple but rather specific equation:

$$C_j^K = V_e^K \phi^K / \tilde{X}_j^K \tag{4.3}$$

C is the estimated total transfer cost as a percentage of total project cost. $\tilde{X}_j^K = X_j^K + \epsilon^K$ where $\tilde{X}_K$ $(\tilde{X}_{Kj} > 0)$ is the Kth independent variable considered $(K = 1, \ldots, 5)$ and $\epsilon^K \neq 0$ for some K.[8] j refers to the jth observation for each K.

With this specification the transfer cost for a project asymptotically approaches a minimum nonzero value as the value of X^K increases. That is, as X^K goes to infinity, C^K goes to V^K. Therefore, V^K is the minimum transfer cost with respect to variable K. However, there is no maximum transfer cost asymptote for the range of the data.

Now the expression for the elasticity of transfer cost with respect to X^K is given by:

$$-\frac{X^K}{C^K} \cdot \frac{dC^K}{dX^K} = -\frac{\phi^K}{\tilde{X}^K} \tag{4.4}$$

Thus, for a given K, and for a specified value of X the elasticity of transfer cost with respect to X is determined by ϕ. Hence, for a given K, the elasticity depends only on ϕ and X.

In order to estimate this function, the log of the arguments is taken

$$C_j^K = V^K e^{\phi^K / \tilde{X}_j^K} \tag{4.5}$$

$$\log C_j^K = \log V^K + \phi^K / \tilde{X}_j^K \tag{4.6}$$

Dummy variables are used to pool the observations across the p projects. Log V_p is the intercept term for the pth project. Inclusion of dummy variables allows the minimum cost asymptote to vary from project to project. Furthermore, it is assumed that ϕ^K is constant across projects $(\phi_p^K = \phi^K)$. These assumptions provide a pooled sample for any given K with dummy intercepts that vary across the p projects. The relevant model for a given K is therefore:

$$\log C_{pj} = \log V_p + \phi / \tilde{X}_{pj} \tag{4.7}$$

Ordinary least square regressions of log C_{pj} on the dummy variables and $1/X_{pj}$ then proceeded for five separate data sets: total transfers, transfers within the chemical and petroleum refining category, transfers in the machinery category, transfers of chemical and petroleum refining technology to developed countries, and transfers of chemical and petroleum refining technology to less developed countries.[9]

The Chow Test[10] (analysis of covariance) of equality between sets of coefficients in two linear regressions revealed that the separation of the sample along industry lines was valid except for the research and development variable. However, there was no statistically valid reason for disaggregating the chemical and petroleum refining subsample according to differences in GNP per capita in the host countries.

The results of the estimation are contained in Table 4-2. The

Table 4-2. Estimated Values of ϕ, and Corresponding t-Statistics, Number of Observations, Degrees of Freedom θ, and r^2

Variable	Chemicals and Petroleum Refining	Machinery
Startups		
ϕ	0.46	0.19
t	(4.23)	(1.76)
n	45	20
r^2	0.92	0.91
θ	25	10
Sales		
ϕ	0.008	0.081
t	(1.17)	(5.18)
n	54	17
r^2	0.88	0.99
θ	35	10
Age		
ϕ	0.04	0.41
t	(1.29)	(2.19)
n	47	21
r^2	0.89	0.94
θ	30	13
Experience		
ϕ	0.007	0.57
t	(0.85)	(6.08)
n	52	13
r^2	0.78	0.91
θ	33	14
R&D/Sales	Total Sample	
ϕ	0.06	
t	(1.58)	
n	59	
r^2	0.90	
θ	30	

estimated equations are characterized by very high r^2 values, but this is mainly a result of the large number of dummy variables relative to the number of observations, and the large across project variation in the data. The intercept term was always highly significant and the coefficients on all the dummies were significantly different from each other.

However, it is the structural variables that are of interest, and a summary table of the various values of ϕ and their significance level to the nearest 0.01 for a one tail test is presented in Table 4-3.

While all of the coefficients are significantly greater than zero at the 0.20 significance level, innovation age, number of startups, size and experience reach at least the 0.05 level in either the chemicals and petroleum refining subsample or the machinery subsample. Further, the variables that are established to be significant in the earlier Phase I analysis are also significant in this analysis. However, some variables that were not attributed significance in Phase I are seen here to have an impact on transfer costs, albeit a small impact.

The elasticity of transfer costs with respect to the independent variables can also be calculated. Elasticity is determined by ϕ and X,

$$\text{i.e.,} -\frac{dc^K}{dX^K} \cdot \frac{X^K}{c} = -\frac{\phi^K}{X^K} \tag{4.8}$$

$-\phi^K/X^K$ will give the point elasticity at X. Average or point elasticities for some typical sample values of X^K are presented in Table 4-4. These elasticity estimates suggest that in the chemical

Table 4-3. Summary of Estimated Values of ϕ

Variable	Chemical and Petroleum Refining	Machinery
Actual startups	0.46	0.19
Significance level	(0.01)	(0.06)
Experience	0.007	0.57
Significance level	(0.20)	(0.01)
Age	0.04	0.41
Significance level	(0.10)	(0.03)
Size	0.008	0.081
Significance level	(0.12)	(0.01)
	Total Sample	
R&D/Sales	0.06	
Significance level	(0.05)	

Table 4-4. Elasticities for Some Typical Sample Values of $\overline{X}^K$

Value of K	Name of $\overline{X}^K$	Chemicals and Petroleum Refining	Machinery
1	number of actual startups	average elasticity	
	1 - 2	0.34	0.14
	2 - 3	0.19	0.08
	3 - 4	0.13	0.05
	9 - 10	0.05	0.02
	14 - 15	0.10	0.01
3	experience of transferee (years)	point elasticity	
	1	0.007	0.57
	2	0.003	0.2ε
	3	0.002	0.19
	10	0.001	0.06
	20	0.000	0.03
4	age of technology (years)	point elasticity	
	1	0.04	0.41
	2	0.02	0.20
	3	0.01	0.14
	10	0.00	0.04
	20	0.00	0.02
5	size (sales value) of transferee	point elasticity	
	1.0	0.008	0.081
	10	0.001	0.008
	20	0.000	0.004
	100	0.000	0.001
	1000	0.000	0.000
2	R&D/Sales of Transferee	Total Sample point elasticity	
	1	0.06	
	2	0.03	
	3	0.02	
	4	0.01	
	5	0.01	
	6	0.01	

category the second startup could lower transfer costs by 34 percent over the first startup, other things being held constant. The corresponding reduction in the machinery category is 14 percent. The corresponding changes in conducting a third startup are 19 percent and 8 percent respectively. All the other elasticities admit of a similar interpretation. For instance, quite large cost reductions follow in the machinery category from more manufacturing experience and older technology. For example, a 1 percent change in the years of manufacturing experience where there has been two years of previous experience could produce a 0.28 percent change in transfer costs in the machinery category.

In general, the estimated data fit a negatively sloped exponential function. Transfer costs asymptotically approach a nonzero minimum cost. Hence, the elasticity declines at a decreasing rate with an increase in X. This has some broad implications for technology transfer. It indicates that, with respect to the variables identified, transfer will be facilitated if the transferee has at least a small endowment of manufacturing experience and R & D type activity, and is large rather than small. Further, costs will be lower if the technology has been commercialized for some time, and if the transferor has already experienced manufacturing startups with this particular technology.

IV.5 COMPARISONS OF PHASE I AND PHASE II RESULTS

First, consider the "number of startups" variable. The Phase I estimates for the chemical industry subsample indicate that it is only the first startup that will lower transfer costs. The level of transfer costs expressed as a percent of total costs is estimated to be 6.73 percentage points higher for the first startup than for subsequent startups. Since the mean value of transfer costs is 10.28 this would indicate a saving of 65 percent relative to the mean. The Phase II results differ in that the data fit a continuous rather than a discrete variable, and the function attributes lower transfer costs to each additional startup. It is not at all surprising that the Phase I analysis did not arrive at this exact same result, given the nature of the data. Accepting the Phase II result that a continuous function does in fact exist, an approximate quantitative correspondence can be demonstrated to exist between the two sets of estimates. The average number of startups for the chemical and petroleum refining category is 4.75. Phase II estimates indicate that five startups will produce cumulated savings of about 76 percent over the first startup. This is a little higher than the 65 percent estimate derived above, but is to be expected since the *ceteris paribus* nature of the estimates will bias the estimates upward. The import of these results is that for chemical petroleum-refining technology transferred abroad without a previous startup, the transfer costs are likely to be substantially higher than the transfer costs of technology that has already been commercialized and undergone several startups. For the machinery category, neither the continuous or the dummy variables for number of startups were significant in Phase I, although in Phase II, U_i turned out to be significant at the 0.06 significance level. However, the elasticity is much less than the elasticity in the chemicals group. The result is entirely consistent with the hypothesis advanced earlier.

Second, consider the years of manufacturing experience of the transferee. This variable turned out to be highly significant in both Phase I and Phase II for the machinery subsample. When the transferee has had only one year of manufacturing experience, a 1 percent change in experience can affect a 0.57 percent change in transfer costs according to the Phase II results. This is 81 percent larger than the estimated change in the chemicals and petroleum refining subsample. Indeed, it is not at all clear that the experience variable has any impact at all in the chemicals and petroleum refining group. In Phase I the variable is significant only at the 0.06 level, while in Phase II it is significant only at the 0.20 level. In both cases, the estimated coefficient is quite small. However, given the capital intensity of the chemicals and petroleum refining industry and the relatively low level of training costs, this is not an altogether surprising result.

Third, consider the age of the technology. Both sets of analysis attributed high levels of statistical significance to this variable in the machinery subsample. However, it was insignificant in the chemical and petroleum subsample in Phase I and only just significant in Phase II. This is entirely in line with the hypothesis presented earlier: namely, in chemicals and petroleum design experimentation does not occur, *ceteris paribus*, with the increasing age of the technology, although it is likely to be an open alternative in industries where the fixed capital costs relative to other costs are relatively low.

Fourth, consider size and the research and development expenditures to sales ratio. Contrary to the Phase I results, size did turn out in Phase II to be significant in the machinery subsample, but the elasticity is quite low over common sample values. The research and development variable is also significant, although the elasticity is again quite low. For the sample data, there is no statistically significant interindustry difference in the impact of this variable. Even when there is no formal R & D expenditure, a percentage point increase in the research and development variable could produce at most a 0.06 percent reduction in costs according to the Phase II results. The effect of the research and development variable could not be identified in the Phase I analysis.

Fifth, consider the number of firms available. Although the Phase II analysis did not include consideration of this variable, it turned out to be significant at the 0.05 level in both industry classifications in Phase I. If this variable is indeed acting as a surrogate for the diffusion of the associated system-specific technology, then the results point to the very considerable impact that the worldwide availability of skills might have on the costs of technology transfer.

What is surprising about these results is not so much the nature of the variables that have been identified, but the quite small impact that some of them seem to have on transfer costs. In particular, although manufacturing experience exhibits a moderately large influence on costs in the electrical and machinery category, it has very little influence on the chemical and petroleum subsample. Perhaps this is not surprising, since learning costs are lower in chemicals and petroleum than in machinery, and it is these learning costs that are most closely influenced by manufacturing experience. Similarly, the age of the technology has almost no affect on transfer costs in chemicals and petroleum refining. Size and research and development to sales ratio have only a very small impact on transfer costs.

Apparently, the dimension of technology transfer costs that is being examined is not determined exclusively by the variables identified. Further research is needed on a broader and larger sample to verify whether these results are a particular characteristic of this sample or whether they are more general. Nevertheless, the results for this sample cast doubt on some of the propositions found in the literature: in particular, there is little evidence for the types of technology in the sample that the existence of a research and development capability by the transferee is a prerequisite for the successful absorption of manufacturing capability. On the other hand, the results identify as important variables rarely mentioned in the literature: for example, the importance of the number of manufacturing startups, age and the extent of diffusion. But clearly more work has to be done on identifying the variables critical to the cost of transfer if understanding of this matter is to advance further.

IV.6 STATISTICAL TESTS: PHASE III

Although the discussion has so far focused on the cost of international technology transfer, there has been no assertion that all of the costs involved are unique to the international transfer of technology. Indeed, in Section II.4 it was pointed out that many of the characteristics and costs of international technology transfer are also common to domestic technology transfer. It is of considerable interest to know how the peculiarly international dimensions of the transfer affect the transfer costs. Unfortunately, foreign and domestic transfers are rarely identical in scope or in timing and so it is not possible to gather data on actually implemented projects at home and abroad that would admit of meaningful comparisons. It was therefore found necessary to fall back on estimates provided by the firms involved in the international transfers. Accordingly, project managers were asked to estimate the dollar amount by which transfer costs would be different if the international transfers in the sample had occurred domestically, holding firm and technology characteristics constant. The procedure was designed to highlight the effects of country characteristics such as differences in language, differences in engineering and measurement standards, differences in economic infrastructure and business environment, and geographical distance from the transferor. For example, suppose a transfer was from the U.S. to a Latin American joint venture, where the partner firm, although small in size and with no research and development capability, had nevertheless been manufacturing a similar line of products for some time. It would then be postulated that the transfer take place to a firm with comparable basic attributes (i.e., size, R & D, previous product lines and quality, years of manufacturing experience) but located in the U.S. Project managers were presented with the relevant scenarios and asked to provide their best estimate of the level of transfer costs under the postulated circumstances. The international component of the transfer cost could be obtained by subtracting the estimated transfer cost from the actual transfer cost associated with the international transfer contained in the sample. The data generated is contained in Table 4-5 and summarized in Table 4-6.

It is immediately clear from Table 4-5 that the difference in cost is not always positive, indicating that in at least some of the cases, it was estimated that the international transfer of an innovation cost less than a comparable domestic transfer.[11] For the sample as a whole, there is on average a small increment of about 7 percent of total transfer costs that could be attributed to the problems involved in transferring abroad. There is nevertheless considerable variation in the data and an explanation of this is called for. Several hypotheses will accordingly be presented and tested. The first is that the difference will be largest when the technology has not been previously commercialized. National boundaries are often surrogates for cultural and language barriers, differences in methods and standards of measurement, and distance from the home country. During first commercialization of a product or process there are generally enormous information flows across the development manufacturing interface. Placing a national boundary at the interface can complicate matters considerably, and escalate the costs enormously. The second hypothesis is that transfers to government enterprises in centrally

Table 4-5.   International Component* of Transfer Cost

Chemicals Petroleum Refining		Machinery	
($ thousands)	As percent of transfer costs for international projects	($ thousands)	As percent of transfer costs
3.03	6.07	35.55	17.88
0.00	0.00	−399.37	−110.93
−12.81	−1.87	50.06	4.93
43.90	31.99	830.70	14.20
0.00	0.00	−4.59	−0.02
5.17	1.42	226.80	14.82
132.75	20.63	.67	1.99
0.00	0.00	−134.40	−13.87
342.00	43.84	34.98	12.95
0.00	−		
0.00	−		
0.00	0.00		
−10.77	−6.66		
−50.16	−8.52		
0.00	−		
637.32	72.60		
−1.33	−1.99		
1,723.81	60.48		
1,370.25	18.45		
524.25	15.69		

*Amount of actual transfer costs attributable to the fact that transfer was international rather than domestic. (Accordingly, negative values indicate that firms estimated that transfer costs would be higher had the transfer been domestic.) In general, these numbers were derived from taking the weighted average of estimated changes in the various identifiable components of transfer costs.

planned economies will involve higher transfer costs. Transferors can expect numerous delays and large documentation requirements.[12] The third hypothesis is that the less the diffusion of the technology, measured as before by the number of other firms possessing the innovation, the greater the positive differential associated with international technology transfer since firm-specific and system-specific technology is relatively more difficult to transfer internationally than domestically. This is not true for general industry technology and basic technology, which can migrate internationally with relative ease. The fourth hypothesis is that whereas, in general, low levels of economic development are likely to add to transfer costs because of inadequacies in the economic infrastructure, in some

**Table 4-6.   International Component as a Percentage of Transfer Costs:
Summary Statistics**

	Total	Chemical and Petroleum Refining	Machinery and Electrical
mean	7.46	14.83	−6.45
minimum	−110.93	−8.52	−110.93
maximum	72.60	72.60	17.88
sample size	26	17	9

circumstances this may be more than offset by lower labor costs.[13]
Lower labor costs can substantially lower excess manufacturing costs
in labor-intensive industries. Accordingly, and since machinery manufacture is relatively labor intensive, the hypothesis is that the level of
GNP per capita in the host country is positively related to the
transfer cost differential in this category but is negatively associated
with the transfer cost differential in the chemicals and petroleum
refining category. To test these hypotheses it was assumed that:

$$D_i = \alpha_0 + \alpha_1 O_{2i} + \alpha_2 U_i + \alpha_3 N_i + \alpha_4 P_i + Z_i \qquad (4.9)$$

where D_i is the "international component" of the transfer costs for
the ith transfer as a percentage of the actual transfer cost of an
international transfer. This variable, therefore, takes the values
presented in columns two and four of Table 4-5. O_{2i} is a dummy
variable that takes the value 1 if the recipient of the ith transfer is a
government enterprise in a centrally planned economy, and zero
otherwise. U_i is a dummy variable that takes the value 1 if there have
been no previous applications (i.e., startups) by the transferring firm
of this technology. N_i is the number of firms identified as possessing
a technology that is "similar and competitive" to the technology
underlying the ith transfer. P_i is the level of GNP per capita of the
host country. Z_i is the random error term for the ith transfer.

Least squares estimates of the αs were obtained for the chemicals
and petroleum and for the machinery subsamples, respectively.[14]
The most satisfactory results were:

$$D_i = \underset{(.91)}{.285} + \underset{(5.01)}{3.84} O_{2i} + \underset{(4.89)}{4.46} U_i \qquad (n = 17, r^2 = .71)$$

$$(4.10)$$

$$D_i = \underset{(-1.96)}{-8.59} - \underset{(-5.98)}{1.39} N_i + \underset{(3.90)}{.005} P_i \quad (n = 9, r^2 = .94)$$

$$(4.11)$$

The hypotheses are to some extent born out by the data, although there are some differences for the two industry classifications identified. In particular, U_i is not significant in the machinery category although the sample is extremely small, and N_i and P_i are not significant in the chemical and petroleum refining category. The small sample size compels caution in the interpretation of these results.[15] However, both N_i and P_i are significant in the machinery category, despite the small number of observations, yet they are insignificant in chemicals and petroleum refining where there are more than twice as many degrees of freedom. This calls for an explanation. The diffusion variable N is taken to indicate the degree to which the requisite skills are generally available. The results of this study suggest that although diffusion lowers the cost of transfer for chemical and petroleum refining transfers, the degree of diffusion has no statistically identifiable impact on the domestic-international transfer cost difference. There is a hint that the relevant skills required are more easily transferred internationally for this industry than they might be for some other industries. One possible explanation of this is that the projects in the chemical and petroleum refining categories are relatively capital-intensive, and it is therefore feasible to embark on extensive prestartup training, abroad if necessary, for a significant percentage of the labor force, since the cost would be relatively low. In contrast, this would not be true for the machinery category, where the training requirements are likely to be more formidable. Furthermore, recall that P_i was hypothesized to have a positive coefficient in the machinery category and a negative coefficient in the chemical and petroleum refining category. However, P_i was not significant in chemicals and petroleum refining. This result suggests that in this industry category, costs of transfer might be independent of the level of economic development of the host country, holding the consideration of first commercialization constant. This highly speculative contention is consistent with the proposition that international technology transfer is no more difficult than domestic transfer when the underlying technology is highly capital-intensive. The perceived reluctance of multinational firms to adapt technology to suit the capital labor requirements of less developed countries could well be rooted to a degree in the desire to avoid escalating transfer costs to unacceptable levels.

NOTES

1. O_{2i} was omitted from the machinery category regression since none of the transfers in this category were to government enterprises in centrally planned economies.

2. Multicollinearity does not appear to be a serious problem in any of the equations. Pairwise correlations amongst the independent variables were never significant at the 0.05 level. The stability of the regression coefficients further suggests that multicollinearity is not serious.

3. If the correct model is the simultaneous equation model $C_i = f(N_i, \ldots)$, $N_i = f(C_i \ldots)$, then to eliminate simultaneous equation bias it would be desirable to use a two stage procedure. A predictor of N could first be obtained by regressing N_i on arguments other than C_i. This could then be used as an argument in the transfer cost regression. However, it was not possible to obtain a good predictor of N using the available cross-section data, so this procedure was not employed. Consistency was sacrificed for efficiency. It is therefore possible that simultaneous equation bias remains in the model. Therefore, the estimates of the parameters may not be consistent.

4. See, for example, J.E. Tilton, *International Diffusion of Technology: The Case of Semiconductors* (Washington, D.C.: The Brookings Institute, 1971), pp. 122-23.

5. The respondents, who were generally project managers, sometimes called on other executives within the firm for verification of the estimates provided.

6. The exception was the "number of previous startups" variable U_i. Since U_i only takes discrete values the hypothesized value of U_i was generally set at $U_1^A + 1$, $U_1^A - 1$, where U_1^A is the actual value of U_i for the ith transfer.

7. The number of firms variable was not included, since at the time the data collection proceeded this variable was considered as an unlikely to contribute to the explanation of transfer costs.

8. $\epsilon \neq 0$ implies a definitional change to some of the K independent variables. The following transformations are made:

$\epsilon_1 = 1$ so that $\tilde{X}_1$ is "number of startups" rather than "number of previous startups."

$\epsilon_2 = 1$ since formal research and development expenditures represented by X_2 do not include expenses for engineerig type activities. Nevertheless, these activities imply the existence of capabilities important for the technology transfer process. A correction factor of +1 percent was therefore added to the variable X_2 (research and development expenditures to sales ratio).

$$\epsilon_3 = \epsilon_4 = \epsilon_5 = 0.$$

9. Less developed countries were defined as those with GNP per capita less than $1,000.

10. See G.C. Chow, "Tests of Equality Between Sets of Coefficients in Two Linear Regressions," *Econometrica* 28:591-605 (July 1960).

11. This seems to be a curious paradox, given that international technology transfer generally augments the transfer activities that have to be performed. Even if the reason is lower labor costs, the identification of the types of transfer for which international transfer costs less than domestic transfer is an issue of importance. An effort to explain the apparent anomalies is attempted below. (An interesting exercise, and one that is not attempted here, would involve computing the cost estimates using first one country's prices and then another's.

It is likely that the separate estimates obtained would exhibit wide dispersion.)

12. See D. Jones, "The 'Extra Costs' in Europe's Biggest Synthetic Fiber Complex at Mogilev, U.S.S.R.," *Worldwide Projects and Installations* 7:30-35 (May-June 1973).

13. The assumption is that lower wage rates will lower labor costs for at least some industries in less developed countries.

14. O_{2i} was omitted from the machinery regression since none of the actual transfers in this catetory were to government enterprises in centrally planned economies.

15. When the second observation on D_i in the machinery category is excluded, and the regression results recomputed, the estimates of the coefficients exhibit considerable instability and the "goodness of the fit" deteriorates. The estimated equation is:

$$D_i = -4.96 - .66N + .003 P_i \qquad (n = 8, r^2 = .45) \qquad (4.12)$$
$$(1.14) \quad (2.40) \quad (1.94)$$

The estimates are nevertheless significant at the 0.05 level for a one tail test.

Chapter Five

Other Determinants of
Total Project Cost

V.1 INTRODUCTION

Transfer costs as defined in this study are only one component of the total cost of establishing a manufacturing facility abroad. The cost of plant and equipment, and the routine engineering associated with plant design and equipment installation, hereafter the "residual" or plant costs, often loom very large in the calculus of the total costs of establishing a manufacturing facility abroad and bringing it on stream. Part of this chapter will be devoted to comparing estimates of the magnitude of variation in the residual costs with the magnitude of variation in transfer costs for international transfers.

The second topic dealt with in this chapter is the extra costs associated with transfer through the market mechanism, as compared with transfer within the various branches of the multinational corporation. In other words, are more resources needed for a given transfer if a licensing agreement is formed with an enterprise that is not wholly owned by the transferor? In particular, Are there extra costs in transferring from a private enterprise to a government enterprise?

Other matters of interest in the process of technology transfer are the size and determinants of the royalty payment or fee that the transferor extracts from the transferee for the rights to utilize the technology in question, and the nature of the tradeoff between cost and time in a technology transfer project. In many cases, the speed with which a project is implemented can have an important impact on the total cost, although the magnitude of the impact is likely to vary from case to case and according to factors that the analysis will attempt to identify.

An attempt will also be made to explain how the transfer activities are shared between the transferor and the transferee. The extent to which transferor size and transferee experience influences the sharing will be examined.

V.2 PLANT COST AND TOTAL PROJECT COST

The cost of performing technology transfer activities is just one component of the total costs of establishing a foreign plant and bringing it on stream. The residual cost—that is, the costs of the plant and equipment, and the associated plant engineering—is generally the largest single component of the project cost, as a cursory examination of the data in Table 3-1 will reveal.

While the analysis in Chapter Four revealed that transfer costs do indeed vary between locations in the home country and locations abroad, it is of interest to consider how the plant cost varies under similar circumstances. Plant cost might vary because of, among other things, differences in factor costs, difference in the capabilities of the local construction industry and distance from major sources of equipment supply. However, although estimates were collected on how the plant costs vary between home and host country, no attempt will be made in this study to achieve a statistical explanation of variation in these costs. Thus, for 28 projects, respondents were able to estimate how, *ceteris paribus*, "plant" cost as defined would differ if the transfer had been conducted within the home country rather than to the actual location abroad. This estimate is used to construct the differential plant cost variable. Table 5-1 shows the relevant cost for 28 projects as estimated by the firm involved. It shows the changes in costs, expressed as a percentage of total actual project costs. A negative sign would indicate that plant cost within the home country would be less than the actual value of the plant cost abroad.

The average change in cost expressed as a percentage of total project costs averages −1.29 percentage points in chemicals and refining, and +2.6 percentage points in the machinery grouping. Hence, while in the former grouping plant costs would on average be lower in the home country, the opposite is true in the machinery category.

Although no attempt is made to explain the very considerable

Table 5-1. Percentage Change in Plant Cost Expressed as a Percentage of Total Project Costs*

Chemicals and Petroleum Refining	Machinery
8.1	0.0
4.3	16.7
8.2	0.0
−13.5	−2.7
0.0	9.8
−3.1	0.0
−1.7	0.0
0.0	0.0
−7.9	0.0
22.5	
−10.0	
0	
−24.2	
−26.7	
0.0	
8.4	
9.1	
0.0	
−1.2	
1.8	
1.8	

*Responses were generated in terms of the percentage change in plant cost. These percentages were then multiplied by the ratio of plant cost to total project cost so as to express the estimate as a percentage of total project cost.

variation in the data,[1] it is of interest to compare, for each project, the sign of this variable with the sign of the variable indicating how transfer costs would change if the transfer had proceeded in the home country rather than at the particular location abroad. In four cases both variables were zero, in four cases the variables had different signs and in 20 cases the variables had the same sign. Whenever signs are different, the plant cost variable has the larger effect in 11 out of the 20 cases.

The import of these results is that in considering the resource cost of international technology transfer, differences in transfer costs among various foreign and domestic locations may be offset by differences in the costs of plant equipment, routine engineering and plant construction.

V.3 RELATIVE PARTICIPATION OF TRANSFEROR AND TRANSFEREE IN TRANSFER ACTIVITIES

The various stages of technology transfer are characterized by a sharing of transfer activities amongst transferor, transferee and engineering contractors. This section will attempt to examine the degree to which transfer activities are shared by transferor and transferee. This will be done by comparing the transfer costs that are attributable to the activities of the transferor and transferee, regardless of how they are eventually allocated. Although this procedure does not allow differentiation according to type of activity, it does give an indication of the degree of resource commitment of each party.

Accordingly, the "participation ratio" R is defined as the ratio of the costs of transfer activities performed by the transferor to the cost of transfer activities performed by the transferee. The following hypotheses may be of use in explaining the variation in this ratio.

First, the larger the transferor, then the more resources at its command and the larger R. In particular, there are likely to be groups within the firm that specialize in international technology transfer. More specialists are therefore likely to be on hand, and the opportunity costs of employing them are likely to be less than the opportunity costs to a small firm that does not have the same degree of international specialization. These factors are likely to manifest themselves in greater relative transfer participation by large transferors.

Second, the experience of the transferee will indicate its ability to absorb new technology without assistance. Hence, the smaller the years of manufacturing experience the transferee has had in the relevant four digit industry, then the greater the relative participation of the transferor in the transfer.

Similarly, the level of economic development of the host country is likely to be a determinant of the amount of transfer assistance that the transferee is likely to require. The less the availability of the requisite infrastructure, then the more assistance that will have to be provided by the transferor.

A fourth consideration is the equity participation of the transferor in the new venture. If the transferor has no equity interest, then it will have an incentive to minimize its participation in the transfer, especially if its services are charged only at direct cost.[2] It will, however, have to fulfill whatever contract obligations are imposed by any licensing agreement that may exist.

The level of transfer costs is also presented as a possible independent variable. The analysis in Chapters Three and Four showed that transfer costs are related to underlying characteristics of the technology. High transfer costs were attributed to what was termed "leading edge" technology, and it is to be expected that the transfer of such technology might require greater participation by the transferor. To test these hypotheses it was assumed that:

$$R_i = \alpha_0 + \alpha_1 S_i + \alpha_2 E_i + \alpha_3 O_{li} + \alpha_4 P_i + \alpha_5 C_i + Z_i \qquad (5.1)$$

where R_i is the transfer costs attributable to activities of the transferor divided by the transfer costs attributable to the transferee; S_i is the sales value of the transferor in millions of dollars; E_i is the number of years of manufacturing experience in the relevant area by the transferee at the time of transfer; O_{li} is a dummy variable that takes the value of 1 if the recipient of the lth transfer is an affiliate of the transferor, and zero otherwise; P_i is the level of GNP per capita in the host country; C_i is the transfer cost as a percentage of total project costs for the lth project; and Z_i is a random error term.

Least squares estimates of the αs were obtained. Variables whose coefficients did not approach significance were eliminated. The results of the most successful equations were:

$$R_i = \underset{(3.98)}{1.47} - \underset{(-2.09)}{.024\,E_i} - \underset{(-1.39)}{.00021\,P_i} + \underset{(2.58)}{.0001\,S_i} \qquad (5.2)$$

$$(n = 19, r^2 = .52)$$

$$R_i = \underset{(3.58)}{1.45} - \underset{(-1.99)}{.024\,E_i} + \underset{(2.89)}{.001\,S_i} \qquad (5.3)$$

$$(n = 19, r^2 = .46)$$

For the 19 projects for which data were available, the mean of R was 1.047 and the variance was 1.048. Dummy variables differentiating the industry grouping were not significant and were therefore omitted. O_{li} and C_i were also insignificant. However, S_i is highly significant. One possible implication is that, assuming the competitive pricing of resources, a licensee with scarce managerial and skill resources might find advantage in buying technology from a large corporation, since it might receive more assistance in the transfer than it might from a smaller transferor. On the other hand, the equations also suggest that more transfer assistance may be provided by the transferor when the transferee is rather inexperienced. A degree of flexibility is clearly apparent in the amount of support that can be supplied by the transferor. The GNP per capita variable, acting as a surrogate for the level of economic development, is almost significant at the 0.10 level. However, even when this variable is included, almost half of the variation in R is unexplained by the equations, indicating that there are omitted variables, errors in variables, or both.

V.4 PROJECT COSTS AND TRANSFER MODES

It was pointed out in Section II.5 that technology transfer can proceed by a variety of modes. A question of very great interest is the relative efficiencies of the various modes. In particular, are total project costs[3] influenced by the level of equity participation of the transferor in the transferee? When there is no equity, the transfer can be considered market-mediated. When there is 100 percent equity participation, the transfer can be considered internal. Are there features of internal transfer—transfer within the multinational firm— that are not shared by market transfer? This section will argue that internal transfers have some efficiency characteristics that at least under some circumstances commend internal transfer over market transfer. Estimates of total project cost according to various modes will be presented and analyzed. It is suggested that the reasons for the superiority of internal over market transfer can be related to the characteristics of the technology and the distribution of the relevant technical knowledge amongst the various parties to the transfer.

Technology transfer is characterized by information asymmetries. One of the parties to the transfer has deeper knowledge of the technology than the other. This problem can affect the efficient allocation of resources by the market, since divergent viewpoints are likely to arise as to how the transfer should proceed. Not all of the contingencies can be written into a licensing agreement. Accordingly, resources may not be allocated as efficiently when transfers occur via the market mechanism (i.e., via licensing agreements with independent firms) rather than via internal transfer to a wholly owned subsidiary. Inefficiency will be manifested in higher project costs.[4]

The properties of the multinational firm that commend internal transfer as a substitute for market transfer appear to be incentives, controls and inherent structural advantages. Because of differences in incentive structures, transfer to a subsidiary attenuates the aggressive advocacy that epitomizes arms length transfer arrangements. Although interests may not be perfectly harmonized between parent and subsidiary, they are at least free of representations of a narrowly opportunistic sort. A further distinct advantage of transfer within the multinational firm is the greater sensitivity and wider variety of control instruments available. Reward and penalty instruments are more refined. Especially relevant is that when disagreements develop, the multinational firm possesses a comparatively efficient conflict resolution machinery. Fiat is frequently a more efficient way to settle minor conflict than is litigation or haggling. Economies of information exchange are a further advantage. It is widely accepted, for instance, that communication with respect to complex matters is facilitated by a common training and experience and if a common code has developed in the process. These are all important considerations with respect to the international transfer of technology. Large information flows are involved, and the litigation machinery at the international level is cumbersome and costly to activate. Of course, the relevance of these arguments for a given transfer will depend on the nature of the innovation and the characteristics of the various parties to the transfer. Besides transfer within the multinational firm, three types of transfer involving different degrees of market transfer can be identified: transfers to joint ventures, transfers to independent private enterprises and transfers to government enterprises in centrally planned economies. To some extent these forms represent a gradation involving increasing loss of control, increasingly divergent incentives and goals, and increasingly difficult problems associated with grievance redress. In addition, greater formality and extra documentation and verification will be required as one progresses from transfer to a wholly owned subsidiary to transfer to a government enterprise in a centrally planned economy.

In order to empirically test some of these notions, estimates were collected on the amounts by which total project costs would change, *ceteris paribus*, according to transfer mode. The firms involved in the transfers outlined in the Appendix were asked to estimate, *ceteris paribus*, the level of total project cost according to whether transfer was to a wholly owned subsidiary, a joint venture in which the transferor owned 49 percent of the equity, a private enterprise in which the transferor possessed no equity or a government enterprise in a centrally planned economy.[5] The data was normalized on total project costs when the transfer was to a wholly owned subsidiary. It is presented in Table 5-2. This data provides support for the contention that internal transfer to a wholly owned subsidiary involves economies not realized by other types of market or semimarket transfer. The magnitude of some of the cost estimates is quite impressive. As the summary statistics in Table 5-3 indicate, the average increment to total project costs is about 5 percent for

Table 5-2. Estimated Percentage Change to Total Project Cost if Transfer is to Other than Wholly Owned Subsidiary

Transfer to:	*Joint Venture* (D_J)	*Independent Enterprise* (D_I)	*Government Enterprise* (D_G)
	0	0	–
	0	0	–
	1	1	3
	10	10	20
	25	25	50
	30	30	35
	3	4	10
	2	2	4
	5	3	5
	10	10	20
	7	7	10
	1	2	7
	0	0	0
	0	5	2
	0	0	–
	0	0	10
	0	1	4
	0	2	9
	0	0	–
	–	1	10
	10	10	12
	1	9	10
	0	0	10
	2	8	10
	0	10	12
	7	15	50
	18	80	95

Table 5-3. Summary Statistics, Estimated Percentage Change in Total Project Costs

Mean	D_J	= 5.07
Standard deviation	D_J	= 8.05
Mean	D_I	= 8.70
Standard deviation	D_I	= 8.05
Mean	D_G	= 17.30
Standard deviation	D_G	= 21.69

transfers to joint ventures, about 9 percent for transfers to non-government enterprises in which there is no equity participation by the transferor and about 17 percent for transfers to government enterprises in which there is no equity participation by the transferor.

Once again, it is apparent that there is considerable variation in the data. For instance, in 11 cases it was estimated that, *ceteris paribus*, transfers to joint ventures would not involve any additional costs over those incurred in transferring to a wholly owned subsidiary, but in six cases the increment was 10 percent or more. Several hypotheses consistent with the earlier arguments can be advanced to explain this variation.[6] It would seem that the loss of equity participation would be most critical when information asymmetries are greatest. This condition will most likely hold when the technology has not been commercialized, for it is then that the transfers are the most complex. Furthermore, the less the manufacturing experience of the transferee, the greater the information asymmetries between the transferor and the transferee, and accordingly, the greater the costs associated with loss of equity control by the transferor. However, it is likely that to some extent the level of actual transfer costs will be a surrogate for these considerations, since in Chapter Four statistical tests demonstrated that a dummy variable for first commercialization and a variable for the experience of the transferee were important determinants of transfer costs. To test these hypotheses it was assumed that:

$$D_{Ji} = \alpha_0 + \alpha_1 C_i + \alpha_2 U_i + \alpha_3 E_i + Z_{iJ} \tag{5.4}$$

$$D_{Ii} = \beta_0 + \beta_1 C_i + \beta_2 U_i + \beta_3 E_i + Z_{iI} \tag{5.5}$$

$$D_{Gi} = \gamma_0 + \gamma_1 C_i + \gamma_2 U_i + \gamma_3 E_i + Z_{iG} \tag{5.6}$$

Ordinary least squares estimates of the αs, βs and γs were generated. A dummy variable was used to pool across the industry groupings. This procedure was adopted since the results of a Chow Test did not suggest that the sample should be divided. The results of the most successful regressions are presented in Tables 5-4, 5-5, and 5-6.

It is immediately apparent that multicollinearity exists amongst the independent variables. In particular, for the 25 observations entering the regression for D_i, the simple correlation coefficients between C_i and the interindustry dummy is 0.81, and the simple correlation coefficient for C_i and U_i is 0.30. Nevertheless, the results clearly delineate one important finding: the transfer abroad of

Table 5-4.   Regression Coefficients and t Statistics in Regression Equations to Explain D_J

Independent Variable	Equation 1	Equation 2	Equation 3
Constant	−0.22 (−0.11)	−1.15 (−0.54)	0.133 (0.08)
Transfer Cost C	0.04 (0.31)	0.29 (3.28)	−
Dummy Variable U for first commercialization	4.60 (1.54)	2.91 (0.94)	4.96 (1.84)
Dummy Variable for machinery projects	9.27 (2.05)	−	10.43 (4.15)
Number of observations	25	25	25
R^2	0.50	0.40	0.50

Table 5-5.   Regression Coefficients and t Statistics in Regression Equations to Explain D_I

Independent Variable	Equation 1	Equation 2	Equation 3
Constant	−1.55 (−0.34)	−0.30 (−0.08)	−2.69 (−0.60)
Transfer Cost C	16 (0.49)	−	0.46 (2.48)
Dummy Variable U for first commercialization	13.41 (2.02)	14.70 (2.45)	11.35 (1.77)
Dummy Variable for machinery projects	11.32 (1.13)	15.40 (2.74)	−
Number of observations	25	25	25
R^2	0.41	0.40	0.37

Table 5-6.   Regression Coefficients and t Statistics in Regression Equations to Explain D_G

Independent Variable	Equation 1	Equation 2	Equation 3
Constant	3.78 (0.60)	3.92 (0.74)	2.17 (0.32)
Transfer Cost C	0.024 (0.05)	−	0.76 (2.73)
Dummy Variable U for first commercialization	10.96 (1.20)	11.10 (1.42)	−
Dummy Variable for machinery projects	27.76 (2.05)	28.36 (3.70)	4.72 (0.51)
Number of observations	21	21	21
R^2	0.47	0.47	0.35

technology not previously commercialized involves enormous additions to total project costs when the transfer does not proceed to a wholly owned subsidiary. Holding the other variables constant, the magnitude of the increment to total project costs is approximately 10-15 percent for projects involving independent firms. Furthermore, the cost increments are greater in the machinery category than in the chemicals and petroleum refining groupings. It seems that the considerable learning requirements in this grouping become especially difficult to achieve when organizational barriers have to be surmounted. This would at least seem to be true for transfers to Eastern European bloc countries where language barriers can be expected to add considerably to the costs of training the labor force and constructing the plant.

V.5 ROYALTY PAYMENTS

Royalty payments are undoubtedly an important component of the cost of technology. Royalty payments are defined in this analysis as the economic rents paid in order to obtain the rights to use intellectual property. They are distinguished from technical service fees, which, although commonly regarded as constituting part of the royalty, are treated in this study as constituting part of transfer costs.

There is undoubtedly a feeling in many host countries that royalty costs are unduly high, and that such costs must be sharply diminished in the future if an adequate flow of new technology toward the developing countries is to be stimulated. It is therefore of interest to examine the level of these costs compared to the other costs that have been identified.

The respondents in this study were presented with the following definition of royalty costs:

> Royalty costs are the payments (including indirect payments such as the markup on technical services and intermediate inputs) made in order to secure access to the technology, that is, access to the drawings and specifications necessary before any enterprise could possibly utilize the technology. Royalty costs do not include technological service fees or any other fees that have already been included in their estimates of engineering, construction, and startup costs. Neither does it include the payments for access to the continuing improvements which may subsequently be made to the original technology.

The respondents were then asked to estimate these costs, or their expected present discounted value if the royalty payments occurred over several years.

Only 14 respondents were able to provide observations on this variable. The other respondents said that the data was company confidential, or that it was too difficult to estimate a future revenue stream. Respondents who encountered the latter problem were entirely in the machine category where royalties are commonly levied as a percentage of annual sales. In the chemical and petroleum refining category, royalties are generally paid as a lump sum at the time the agreement is consummated. Hence, it was much easier for these respondents to provide the requested data. Table 5-7 shows the relevant costs for 14 projects.

It is clear that even within the chemicals and petroleum industry classification, there is considerable variation from project to project in the level of royalty payments, expressed as a percentage of total project costs. Royalty payments, representing the price for the right to utilize industrial knowledge, will, like any other price, be determined by supply and demand. However, the peculiar nature of the market for technology makes the identification of the arguments entering the demand and supply functions rather difficult. Consider first the supply function. Assuming the firm's price technology as the average cost of producing and transferring it, then the initial research and development costs are likely to enter the individual firm's supply function.[7] The supply cost to the firm may also be influenced by a premium associated with the risks of disclosure. With each sale of technology there is a chance that the transferee might use the

Table 5-7.   Royalty Payments as a Percentage of Total Project Costs: 14 Projects in Chemicals and Refining

3.5
19.8
19.3
6.2
27.7
1.5
2.5
1.7
20.8
19.8
2.5
3.0
3.0
0.4

mean royalties   = 9.4
standard deviation = 9.6

technology in a manner prejudicial to the supplier firm. One "undesirable" outcome would be unanticipated competition from the recipient firm itself through its successful utilization of the disclosed technology. The unauthorized, purposeful or inadvertent disclosure of the technology to third parties[8] either during or after the transfer would be viewed similarly by the supplier. The industry supply function will also, of course, be influenced by the number of firms possessing and willing to license the same or similar technology. Second, consider the demand for the technology. This is likely to be a function of the expected profitability of the process or product. Absolute profitability will increase with the level of output of the production facility, assuming profitability on initial units and assuming a degree of demand elasticity for the product.

Unfortunately, the data base assembled for this study does not allow direct testing of the price formation model suggested above, either in the structural form or in a reduced form. However, surrogates are available that shed some light on the hypotheses advanced above. In particular, data are available on the number of firms possessing similar and competitive technology, although it is not known if these potential suppliers would be willing to license their technology. Some firms have policies that prohibit licensing of what they regard as their "gemstone" technology. However, if one firm is prepared to license the technology then there are strong reasons why its competitors might also be willing to license their competitive technology. Therefore, one would expect the number of firms variable defined earlier in this study to be an acceptable surrogate for the number of firms prepared to license the technology. Furthermore, and assuming that size of investment is a surrogate for capacity, the risk premium associated with unauthorized disclosure or unanticipated rivalry is likely to manifest itself in proportionally lower royalties for larger plants, assuming that risk is independent of production capacity.

In order to test this hypothesis, it was assumed that

$$\overline{R}_i = \alpha_0 + \alpha_1 N_i + \alpha_2 / I_i + Z_i \tag{5.7}$$

where $\overline{R}_i$ is the royalty payment expressed as a percentage of the total cost of the project; N_i is the number of firms identified as possessing a technology that is "similar and competitive" to the technology underlying the ith transfer; I_i is the plant and equipment cost (Stage C cost as defined in Chapter II) of the ith project; and Z_i is a random error term.

Least squares estimates of the αs were obtained, the results being

$$\overline{R}_i = 14.02 - \underset{(5.29)}{} \underset{(-3.13)}{.85\,N_i} + \underset{(2.03)}{6884184/I_i} \tag{5.8}$$

$$r^2 = .63$$
$$n = 14$$

All of the observations are in the chemical and petroleum industry grouping. A dummy variable introduced to indicate whether the transfer was to an affiliate or not was introduced and withdrawn because it failed to be statistically significant.

The above very simple equation explains 63 percent of the variation in the dependent variable. The number of competitors variable is highly significant, pointing to the fact that the availability of other sources of supply is an important variable in explaining the royalty payment. Furthermore, projects with larger investments in plant and equipment have lower costs than smaller projects. This might be interpreted as indicating that the plants with larger capacity and output are in a better position to spread the risk premium levied as compensation for the risks associated with possible disclosures of the technology.[9]

It is clear from the descriptive statistics and from the equation that the royalty costs can be quite high, particularly if there are few alternative sources of supply. For the chemical and petroleum industry, the mean value is close to the mean value of the transfer cost. For the machinery category, royalties are generally expressed as a percentage of sales, and this percentage is generally from 2 percent to 10 percent.[10] Under the same normalization procedure as used in chemicals and petroleum, it is likely that R_i will be greater than 100 percent. Three respondents in the machinery category provided estimates that ranged from 150 to 310 percent. Since these figures were based on estimated future sales and an assumed discount rate of 10 percent, these observations were not included in the sample.

It is apparent that royalties are a very real component of the cost of technology, at least from the point of view of the recipient firm. The firm that has developed the knowledge should be able to demand a large share of the profits: "ideally" all except a competitive return on the capital invested. Since the profits that can be generated from a successful technical innovation are often very considerable, it seems pertinent to ask what sets the limit on the level of royalty costs. One possible explanation is that the costs of transfer set the limit. When transfer costs are large, there may be little extra return to squeeze.[11] Nevertheless, while transfer costs and royalties provide formidable obstacles to the flow of information across enterprise and national boundaries, it is clear that the costs are far from absolute. Technology transfer is costly, but there are many circumstances when it is sufficiently profitable to warrant its conduct.

V.6 TIME-COST TRADEOFFS: GENERAL CONSIDERATIONS

An innovation and the technology required to implement it can often be transferred abroad more quickly if more resources are spent during the course of the transfer. Time-cost tradeoffs in research and development, and in innovation, have previously been studied by economists.[1,2] However, the time-cost tradeoff has never been estimated for technology transfers, domestic or international.

Time-cost tradeoffs in international technology transfer are of interest for several reasons. The ability to transfer technology quickly in response to changing market requirements is of considerable importance to the multinational firm, although there may be several alternative routes by which a new foreign market can be supplied. It may be supplied by export from the parent or another subsidiary, or it may be supplied by means of a licensing or patent agreement with independent enterprises. Licensing, however, may also involve substantial technology transfer and the establishment of a new manufacturing facility abroad. On the other hand, if the potential licensee is already manufacturing similar products, the licensing agreement might merely imply minimal adaptation to existing facilities and very little technology transfer. While licensing to an already existing manufacturer may be the least cost method of meeting a new demand in the shortest time, this is unlikely to be a viable alternative if the potential licensee is a competitor or potential competitor. Further, the nature of the innovation may be such that an entirely new manufacturing facility is needed, in which case there may be little advantage to licensing as a mechanism to respond swiftly to changing market requirements.

Hence, on many occasions it could well appear to the multinational firm that the most promising route for bringing a new product or process to a foreign location in the shortest possible time is by rapidly completing a transfer of the relevant technology to an affiliate rather than by switching to a different mode of technology transfer. On the other hand, if technology transfer is felt appropriate but there is no great urgency attached to the accomplishment of the transfer, cost minimization may indicate that the project proceed at a slower speed.

There are a number of ways in which a project can be speeded up.

More resources can be spent on prestartup training of the labor force so that the plant can be started up as quickly as possible. More instruction and supervision can be supplied, or skilled operators can be brought in lock, stock and barrel from another installation—but usually only at very great expense. During construction the project is largely at the mercy of vendors for equipment and parts, so there is not a great deal that can be done to speed up the project during this phase. Greater efforts can be made to secure quicker delivery of key pieces of equipment. For instance, there might be some payoff from greater expediting expenditures. Sometimes it may be possible to buy shop time before the engineering has been completed. Further, purchasing materials from the warehouse rather than the factory will cut lead times, but only at a considerable expense. The engineering may be speeded up by applying more engineers to the job. However, the biggest problem in attempting to speed up a project is the long lead times involved for equipment. These vary with the business cycle and other factors which can be regarded as essentially exogeneous as far as most firms are concerned. International projects are further constrained by worldwide shipping, so that the degree by which time can be saved on an international project is clearly quite limited, especially for the construction phase.

Data pertaining to the time-cost tradeoff was obtained from interviews with corporate and project managers. The transfer process was considered to begin when the board of directors or other executive group formally approved the project. Using the actual cost and the actual time for the project as a reference point, respondents were asked to estimate the percentage change in the actual cost that would result from specified percentage changes in the actual time. In addition, the respondent was asked to estimate the minimum possible time in which the project could have been completed. Usually five observations on time and cost were obtained for each project, in addition to the actual time and cost.

There is widespread agreement that the time-cost tradeoff function is likely to be negatively sloped and convex over a certain range, but that it will be positively sloped beyond that range (see Figure 5-1).[13] BC is regarded as the normal range. Points right of C are considered highly unlikely because they most likely represent suboptimal behavior. However, it is of interest to note that for 13 of the projects in the sample, costs would increase if expected time were doubled. Clearly, points to the right of C would never be chosen *ex ante* under normal circumstances. However, it is possible that a firm could realize *ex post* that the transfer did in fact proceed at a point to the right of C. Indeed, some respondents were quick to point out

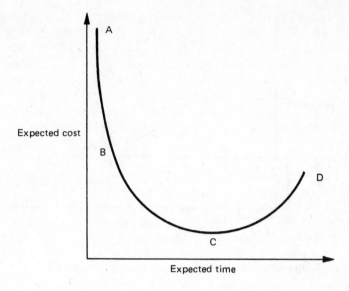

Figure 5-1. Transfer Possibility Curve

that with respect to international technology transfer, points to the right of C could be easily encountered.

V.7 ESTIMATION OF THE TIME-COST TRADEOFF

It was decided to estimate the downward sloping portion of the time-cost tradeoff. Therefore, points to the right of C were excluded from the data base. Data were made available for 20 of the 29 projects in the sample.

To begin with, the assumption is made that the downward sloping section of the time-cost tradeoff can be represented by:

$$C = Ve^{\frac{\phi}{(t/\alpha) - 1}} \qquad (5.9)$$

where C is the expected cost of the project, t is the expected time, and v, α and ϕ are parameters that vary from project to project. Figure 5-2 shows the nature of this function. It is convex and has both time and cost asymptotes.

Since C approaches v as t becomes larger, v can be considered the minimum expected cost of the project. Since t approaches α as C becomes larger, α can be considered the minimum expected time to

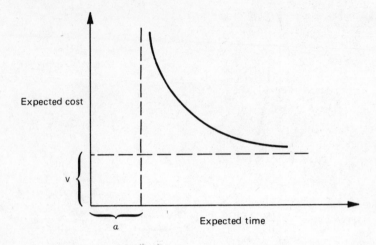

Figure 5-2. Graphical Representation of Equation 5.9

complete the innovation. The elasticity of cost with respect to time, $-\dfrac{dc}{at}\dfrac{t}{c}$, is equal to

$$\frac{\phi(t/\alpha)}{[(t/\alpha)-1]^2}$$

Thus, for a given value of t/α, the elasticity of cost with respect to time is determined by ϕ. If the above equation holds, then

$$lnC = lnv + \phi[(t/\alpha - 1)]^{-1} \qquad (5.10)$$

Since direct estimates of α have been obtained from the respondents for each project, estimates of v and ϕ can be obtained by regressing lnC on $1/(t/\alpha - 1)$. The results are summarized in Table 5-8.

In general, it can be said that the goodness of fit is acceptable, although in each case the number of observations is very small.

Using the estimated value of ϕ, the elasticity of cost with respect to time can be calculated for a given value of t/α. Table 5-9 represents the results of this calculation. t was set at its actual value.

The results show that in 15 out of the 20 cases, strategies aimed at shaving the actual time by 1 percent would raise costs by more than 1 percent. Apparently, the time-cost tradeoff function for international technology transfer is much more elastic than the time tradeoff function for innovation.[14]

Table 5-8. Estimates of V, α and ϕ: 20 International Projects

Project	v	α	ϕ	r^2
1	260	9	0.024	0.61
2	1,998	20	0.068	0.69
3	3,964	14	0.065	0.99
4	796	11	0.146	0.99
5	578	32	0.174	0.90
6	1,808	28	0.070	0.98
7	9,228	24	0.089	0.55
8	3,197	15	0.030	0.95
9	111	3	0.279	0.96
10	459	10	0.072	0.94
11	1,615	21	0.007	0.82
12	11,395	30	0.119	0.96
13	29,971	61	0.028	0.98
14	2,470	20	0.115	0.95
15	654	12	0.053	0.94
16	3,901	22	0.122	0.91
17	12,100	27	0.560	0.79
18	4,745	36	0.185	0.78
19	10,872	36	0.021	0.97
20	620	17	0.041	0.97

Table 5-9. Estimates of Elasticity of Cost with Respect to Time at Actually Realized Values of t/α

Point Elasticity	1.00-1.25	1.26-1.50	t/α 1.51-1.75	1.76-1.75	Total
0-0.50	1	0	1	0	2
0.51-1.00	2	1	0	0	3
1.01-1.50	1	1	0	1	3
1.51-2.00	4	0	0	0	3
2.01-2.50	3	1	0	0	3
2.51-3.00	1	1	0	0	2
3.01-3.50	2	1	0	0	3
over 3.50	1	0	0	0	1
Total	13	5	1	1	20

V.8 DETERMINANTS OF THE ELASTICITY OF COST WITH RESPECT TO TIME

The elasticity of cost with respect to time varies considerably from project to project. An attempt will be made to explain variation in the elasticity estimates evaluated at the point on the tradeoff function where the expected time to conduct the transfer is equal to the actual time taken.

The first hypothesis to be advanced is that the elasticity will be lower the longer the duration of Stage A relative to the other stages. Stage A can generally be telescoped if the need arises. It involves relatively low level activity (see Chapter Two), which can be intensified relatively easily if management decides that this would be worthwhile. The converse of this hypothesis is that the engineering, construction, installation and startup can be telescoped, but only at a relatively greater expense.

The second hypothesis is that the elasticity will be lower if the technology has been applied previously. If there has been at least one startup, then attention can be directed away from problems of the technology per se to problems of transfer: i.e., attention can be directed to ways of streamlining and expediting the transfer. A strategy to speed up the first transfer by maximizing overlap will present colossal problems because of the uncertainty involved.

The third hypothesis is that the elasticity will also be determined by the size of the primary transfer agent. The primary transfer agent is defined to be the enterprise with the controlling equity in the new venture. Thus, the transferor will be the primary agent if the transfer is to a subsidiary, but the transferee will be the primary agent if the transfer is to an independent enterprise. The primary agent is generally the entity that will hire the engineering contractors and authorize the bidding on pieces of equipment. It will have the responsibility of expediting the transfer. On a priori grounds it seems reasonable to hypothesize that the larger the size of the primary agent, the greater their command over resources, and hence, the greater their ability to speed the transfer at lower costs than a smaller firm could achieve. On the other hand, and insofar as speeding up an innovation requires a certain flexibility of approach, a larger organization may be handicapped by inertia and a more complex decision-making procedure. Even reaching agreement on how to proceed will take longer if more people and a longer chain of command is involved.

Finally, the elasticity may be influenced by total project costs. On a priori grounds it seems reasonable to hypothesize that because large projects require more coordination and integration of different tasks, they may be more costly to speed up than smaller projects.

To test these hypotheses it was assumed that

$$\epsilon_i = \alpha_0 + \alpha_1 A_i + \alpha_2 \tilde{C}_i + \alpha_3 \tilde{S}_i + \alpha_4 \tilde{U}_i + Z_i \qquad (5.11)$$

where ϵ_i is the estimated elasticity of cost with respect to time calculated at the actual time taken for the transfer; A_i is the percentage of total time allocated to Stage A (as defined in Chapter Two); $\tilde{C}_i$ is the total cost of the ith project; $\tilde{S}_i$ is the sales volume of the primary transfer agent for i^{th} transfer; $\tilde{U}_i$ is a dummy variable that takes the value 1 if this transfer represents the first application of the technology, and zero otherwise; Z_i is a random error term.

Ordinary least squares estimates of the s yielded:

$$\epsilon_i = -2.29 - 2.17\,A_i - .000056\,\tilde{C}_i + .00012\,\tilde{S}_i + .93\,\tilde{U}_i$$
$$(10.45)\quad(2.63)\qquad(3.31)\qquad\quad(2.05)\qquad(2.63)$$

$$(r^2 = .64,\ n = 20)\qquad\qquad(5.12)$$

All of the variables are significant. However, the coefficient of C_i has a negative sign, which is contrary to the hypothesis advanced earlier. Apparently the larger the project, the lower the absolute value of the elasticity estimate calculated at the actual time taken for the transfer. One possible explanation is that although total time could be reduced, there is little incentive to shave since the extra revenue from earlier sale of product may be less than the extra cost of achieving it. If the marginal revenue following from quicker transfer is low, profit maximization will compel the transfer to proceed where both the elasticity and therefore the marginal cost of time reduction is relatively low.

Although these results are not particularly surprising, the examination and estimation of the time-cost tradeoff for international technology transfer projects has been instructive for several reasons. First, it points to the relatively elastic nature of the tradeoff: small changes in the time taken have relatively large influences on the cost. Furthermore, while only the negatively sloped portion of the time-cost tradeoff was estimated, 13 cases were encountered where costs would increase if expected time were doubled. The fact that the elasticity is nonzero suggests that good project management to ensure that the project proceeds at the optimum speed is likely to be of critical importance. Effort must be directed to ensuring that the project proceed according to schedule. Thorough checking and close supervision and inspection are likely to be a part of this. Commencing the project with incomplete designs or inadequate knowledge of local conditions and regulations may well involve opportunity costs, or cost overruns if the project is forced onto the positively sloped portion of the time-cost tradeoff.

NOTES

1. For a discussion of factors that might be important, see the following: John Gallagher, "Efficient Estimation of Worldwide Plant Costs," *Chemical Engineering* (June 2, 1962), pp. 196-202; Robert Johnson, "Costs of Overseas Plants," *Chemical Engineering* 76:146-52 (March 10, 1969); and Yen-Chen Yen, "Estimating Plant Costs in the Developing Countries," *Chemical Engineering* 79:89-92 (July 10, 1972).

2. Direct costs to the transferor are assumed to be less than opportunity costs for many types of transfer activity.

3. The focus of attention is the affect of transfer mode on total project cost rather than just the transfer cost component of total project costs. It is argued that the extra costs are of a transactional nature and influence all project costs, including transfer costs.

4. This is a particular case of a more general problem involved in the workings of the market economy. See K.J. Arrow, "The Organization of Economic Activity," in *The Analysis and Evaluation of Public Expenditures: The PPB System*, 1, Joint Economic Committee, 91st Cong., Washington, D.C., 1969, pp. 54-56.

5. Four of the 27 firms providing data did not have experience with transfers to this type of government enterprise, and accordingly they were not able to provide estimates on this class of transfer.

6. These hypotheses are simultaneously addressed to variation in D_J, D_I and D_G (these variables are defined in Table 5-2).

7. However, the market for an innovation seems to possess many of the attributes likely to facilitate price discrimination. This is a small numbers market, and it is quite legitimate to write and enforce agreements prohibiting the arbitrage of a given innovation. Furthermore, discovery of the potential licensees' demand for an innovation may not be too difficult to estimate if the transferor already has knowledge of consumers' preferences for the final product. In any case, the small numbers attributes of the market for innovations means that it is not prohibitive to devote considerable effort toward discovery of the relevant preferences or demands. Accordingly, the transactions costs associated with perfect price discrimination may be relatively trivial.

8. For example, the engineering contractor might learn enough about the technology to make invention around the patent an easy task.

9. On the other hand, and since plant and equipment costs are correlated with total project costs (which are used to normalize royalty payments), the relationship between I_i and R_i could be merely a statistical artifact.

10. In the G.R. Hall and R.E. Johnson study, "Transfers of United States Aerospace Technology to Japan," in R. Vernon, ed., *The Technology Factor In International Trade* (New York: National Bureau of Economic Research, 1970), pp. 340-41, royalties for the F-104J airframe were approximately 6.9 percent of average per unit production costs, and 4.7 percent for the F-104J engine. Royalty payments were twice technical assistance payments for the airframe technology and about one-tenth technical assistance payments for the engine technology.

11. Arrow, for example, remarks on what he regards as the relatively low level of royalty costs. To Arrow it is not clear that the profits from exploiting one's own invention are appreciably greater than those derived from the use of others' knowledge, and this calls for an explanation. See K. Arrow, "Comment," in Universities—National Bureau Committee for Economic Research, *The Rate and Direction of Inventive Activity* (Princeton: Princeton University Press, 1962), p. 355.

12. See, for example, Mansfield et al., *Research and Innovation in the Modern Corporation* (New York: W.W. Norton, 1971), chs. 4 and 7.

13. For analogous treatment of the development possibility curve, see F.M. Scherer, "Government Research and Development Programs," in R. Dorfman, ed., *Measuring the Benefits of Government Expenditures* (Washington, D.C.: The Brookings Institution, 1965).

14. See Mansfield et al., where in most cases the cost increase was estimated to be less than 1 percent.

Chapter Six

Conclusion

VI.1 INTRODUCTION

In this chapter consideration is given to the implications of the findings presented in the preceding chapters. Of course, the implications drawn must be regarded as at most suggestive, since the sample is quite small and the data is not without deficiencies. Although there will be some overlap, the implications will be considered under four headings: implications for the understanding of the resource cost of technology transfer, public policy toward technology transfer, implications for the study of international trade and investment, and implications for the study of multinational enterprise.

VI.2 THE TECHNOLOGY TRANSFER PROCESS: CHARACTERISTICS AND COSTS

Economists' understanding of the process of international horizontal technology transfer has until recently been extremely limited. Knowledge of the process has not extended much beyond a realization that it does indeed occur, and that the consequences are important. Very little has been known about the nature of the resources used and the costs involved. In lieu of evidence to the contrary, it has sometimes been argued that the costs of transfer are trivial, at least compared to the cost of developing the innovation. This characterization has been challenged by the study, as well as by other writers. Indeed, there is a suggestion that the costs involved and the nature of the transfer activity are not too different from the process of R & D itself. Both involve a substantial commitment of resources and a sequence of overlapping stages of activity. Progression through these stages results in a reduction in uncertainty. The transfer process and the R & D process can both be speeded up if a substantial increment of resources is committed. Nevertheless, there are important differences. R & D involves the intensive utilization of research scientists and engineers, while the transfer of technology depends only incidentally on the services of research personnel. Competent manufacturing engineers and project managers are the key to the success of technology transfer. Furthermore, whereas an R & D project is performed but once, the activities constituting technology transfer are likely to be repeated on many occasions, presenting opportunities for "learning by doing" in technology transfer.

VI.3 PUBLIC POLICY TOWARD TECHNOLOGY TRANSFER

The results of this study indicate substantial resources must be utilized not only to transmit technical information but also to ensure its successful absorption. Furthermore, these costs will vary considerably, more especially according to the number of previous applications of the innovations and to how well the innovation is understood by the parties involved. Accordingly, it is entirely inappropriate to regard technology as something that once acquired by one firm can be made available to others at zero social cost. Even aside from questions relating to the generation of new technology, it need not be socially efficient for all firms to have absolutely free access to a new innovation.[1] Substantial fees may often have to be charged to reflect the resource cost of transmitting technical information.

Furthermore, since substantial investment is required to effectively utilize an innovation, there may be circumstances under which governments might want to protect the transferees' investment in technology transfer as well as the transferors' investment in R & D. In particular, since costs of transfer decline with each application, first imitators might be disadvantaged relative to later imitators because they have to incur higher transfer costs.[2] In order that imitation proceed at the socially desirable rate, a degree of patent protection to licensors and licensees might be called for under some circumstances, assuming that the transferor is not a perfect price discriminator and that the technology fees reflect the costs of transmitting the technology. In addition, the results suggest that the magnitude of transfer costs vary across industries, so that any policy prescription should attend to the differences that exist in the technology transfer process.

The results of this study also have some bearing on the transfer costs associated with separating production from development. In particular, they indicate that the concept of directed licensing[3] is most likely to be a useful device for lowering procurement costs when production runs are long enough to permit second sourcing. The especially high cost of transfer before first application is likely to favor the developer for production of initial units. That is, the developer will possess a first mover advantage. However, since transfer costs decline with each startup and with time, it is clear that transfer costs will be lowered once the developer has commenced the first production run. Accordingly, the competitive stance of other firms with manufacturing experience in the relevant area is likely to be enhanced if two or more production runs seem possible. Furthermore, although it may be politically unrealistic for weapons systems procurement, international bidding could well lower procurement costs for some innovations. The results of this study suggest that the "extra" cost in transferring abroad is by no means formidable, especially if it occurs after first application. Indeed, there is evidence to suggest that foreign firms, or U.S. multinationals with production facilities abroad, could well be in a position to outbid domestic rivals in some circumstances.

VI.4 IMPLICATIONS FOR INTERNATIONAL TRADE AND INVESTMENT

The literature on international trade theory has only recently given recognition to the fact that it is increasingly inappropriate to ignore interrelations between output and input flows. Classical international trade theory has generally assumed that commodities could be shipped from one country to another, but the factors or production either could not or would not migrate internationally. However, as Baldwin[4] has pointed out, it is common to observe the international firm weighing the alternatives of producing a particular commodity in one country and then shipping it to the market of another country, or transferring technology to this latter country and manufacturing the product there. The specific manner chosen to meet the demand depends not only on relative production costs, but also on the relative costs of transferring inputs and outputs. To the extent that the cost of transferring inputs is discussed at all in classical theory, the focus of attention is usually on transport costs. Knowledge is an important input in the production process, but it is rarely discussed. Nevertheless, if consideration is given to establishing a manufacturing facility abroad based on imported technology, knowledge will have to be transferred, and the costs of transferring knowledge will have some import on the decision. This is not to imply that the cost of transferring knowledge is the deciding factor in international technology transfer and international investment at the macro level.[5] Rather, the suggestion is that any attempt to explain the nature and differential patterns of technology transfer at the micro level ought to exhibit awareness of the factors identified as influencing the costs of transferring particular technologies to particular enterprises.

Furthermore, the findings of this study can be seen as providing some small embellishments to the product cycle model,[6] which posits that a newly developed product will first be manufactured in the U.S.A. because of the need for flexibility and swift and effective communication on the part of the producer with customers and suppliers. The product in time becomes standardized, production costs begin to play a greater role and transfer abroad becomes more likely. Contained within this reasoning is an argument that technology transfer costs are high when the technology has not been previously commercialized, but decline thereafter, and that this progression influences the timing of technology transfer. The results of this study provide support for this notion since transfer costs were seen to decline after first application, and with the further diffusion of the technology. However, interindustry differences appear to be very great, and it is likely that in some industries the product cycle model is inapplicable in its present form. For instance, many of the considerations mentioned above are of little consequence for the transfer of process innovations, although the costs involved in separating development from production may still be large enough to delay international transfer for some time after first application. Furthermore, the magnitude of the additional costs involved in conducting international transfer before first application was in several cases revealed to be insufficiently large to deter first application abroad in affiliates of the multinational firm.

VI.5 IMPLICATIONS RELATING TO THE MULTINATIONAL FIRM

The international transfer of technology by the multinational firm involves the utilization of a diverse set of skills and resources. The multinational firm seems to be an instrument particularly well suited for bringing this diverse set of requirements together. By employing a variety of modes and methods, the international firm seems able to effectively transfer many different kinds of technology under many different circumstances. For any given mode of transfer, the multinational firm seems able to adjust its degree of participation in the transfer as the need arises. Substitution possibilities amongst the resources of the transferor, the transferee and the independent engineering and construction contractors can be exploited to the fullest. The demonstrated versatility in selecting different modes of transfer and different methods of transfer, and versatility in adjusting the relative participation of the parties to the transfer, can provide the basis for the rapid diffusion of modern technology and the efficient utilization of resources. Indeed, the rather surprising discovery that for the sample as a whole the extra costs of international transfer are perceived as quite modest could very well be a reflection of this efficiency attribute of the multinational firm.

The results also yield some managerial implications for firms involved in international technology transfer. While the manufacturing experience, size and R & D to sales ratio of the transferee were identified as statistically significant determinants of transfer costs for the sample, there was also evidence to suggest that any firm moderately matured in these dimensions is a good candidate to absorb the technology at relatively low cost. It is not clear, for instance, that supergiant firms have any advantage in this respect over moderately sized firms. Nor is it clear that highly research-intensive firms have more than a slight advantage over firms with a minimal commitment to research and development. However, manufacturing experience is important, but more particularly in some industries than in others. The results nevertheless delineate some characteristics of firms that might possibly make them acceptable licensees or joint venture partners, but the possession of these characteristics is by no means compelling. In addition, there is evidence that the licensee can expect greater assistance the larger the transferor. This could well be a reflection of the greater absolute slack in the larger firm and accordingly the lower opportunity cost of assisting in the transfer activities.

One further implication is that since transfer costs decline with each application of a given innovation, technology transfer is a decreasing cost activity. This can be advanced as an explanation for the specialization often exhibited by engineering firms in the design and installation of particular turnkey plants. This is a characteristic particularly noteworthy of the petrochemical industry, where the underlying technology is often state of the art. Assuming demand is not completely inelastic, a transferor and contracting engineer with many applications of a given innovation to their credit are often able to transfer at lower cost and higher profit than competitors without this experience. Under the circumstances, profitability in licensing for an individual firm and contractor might well be enhanced if licensors can secure more transfer agreements than rival firms are able to secure. Declining transfer costs under these circumstances open possibilities for higher royalties with each subsequent transfer.

The results of this study also provide some new evidence relating to the efficiency attributes of the multinational firm in technology transfer. Although there were no observations available to allow comparisons of transfer costs by organizations other than multinational firms, it was possible, however, to collect estimates on variation in total project costs according to the organizational form of the transferee (subsidiary, joint venture, independent enterprise, government enterprise). The results suggest that total project costs increase considerably as control declines. In particular, transfers to government enterprises involve substantial increments to total project costs. Apparently equity participation is important if total project cost is to be minimized. This was in line with the contention that transfer can be facilitated within the multinational firm because of economies realized in transactions costs and the superior incentive and control devices that the firm possesses and has available for use over internal transaction, but not over market transactions. These considerations are particularly important when information asymmetries exist, which is the usual circumstance in technology transfer.

Yet even if the multinational firm is a relatively efficient instrument for allocating world resources, the returns for this endeavor may not be perceived as improving world welfare. In particular, royalty payments have received only limited attention in this study, being treated as economic rents received for the right to utilize intellectual property, but these payments will nevertheless have important effects on the world distribution of income and the decisions of nonaffiliates to utilize available technology. Clearly the multinational firm will always be perceived as presenting a mixed bag of attributes.

NOTES

1. For examples of a conflicting view, see H.G. Johnson, "The Efficiency and Welfare Implications of the International Corporation," in C.P. Kindleberger, ed., *The International Corporation* (Cambridge, Mass.: M.I.T. Press, 1970), pp. 35-36, and W. Leontief, "On Assignment of Patent Rights on Inventions Made Under Government Research Contracts," *Harvard Law Review* 7:492-97 (January 1964). Leontief suggests an equivalence between the marginal cost involved

in utilizing a highway, and the marginal costs of utilizing an innovation. Furthermore, his exhortation to the effect that when dynamic considerations are irrelevant (when technology is generated, for instance, under government contract to the private sector) technology ought to be available to all free of charge is rather a careless prescription since the costs of transmitting technology may not be zero.

2. Higher transfer costs may or may not be offset by the monopoly rents accrued before subsequent imitators drove price down to marginal cost.

3. Directed licensing involves the granting of development contracts (such as for weapons procurement by the government) obliging the recipient to transfer the resultant technology to whomever the government designates at agreed upon prices during any or all production runs. For an elaboration of this concept, see Gregory Carter, "Directed Licensing: An Evaluation of a Proposed Technique for Reducing the Procurement Cost of Aircraft" (Santa Monica, Cal.: The Rand Corporation, R-1604-PR).

4. R.E. Baldwin, "International Trade in Inputs and Outputs," *American Economic Review* 60:430-34 (May 1970).

5. Market size has been identified as important here. See, for instance, A.E. Scaperlanda and L.J. Mauser, "The Determinants of U.S. Direct Investment in the E.E.C.", *American Economic Review* 59:558-68 (September 1969).

6. See Raymond Vernon, "International Investment and International Trade in the Product Cycle," *Quarterly Journal of Economics* 80:190-207 (May 1966).

Appendixes

Appendix A:
Twenty-nine Cases

Presented below are some observations and comments on each of the 29 transfer projects on which data were obtained. The purpose in presenting this material is to give the reader a deeper appreciation for the kinds of technology transferred and the nature of the main actors in the transfer process.

Case 1

A U.S. multinational transferred to a Brazilian firm the technology required to manufacture automotive finishes. A highly complex process was involved, but the transfer imposed few problems as it had been performed several times previously. The startup proceeded in two phases. The plant was first started on imported materials and then switched to local materials. This made the startup problems more manageable.

Case 2

A U.S. multinational transferred to its French subsidiary the technology required to manufacture automotive finishes. The transferor considered the particular process to be the best available in the industry. There were several false starts in the transfer, and the transferor attributed this to attempts by the transferee to modify the technology, motivated by an NIH complex. The program eventually succeeded when these attitudinal problems were resolved.

Case 3

A large U.S. multinational, with sales of several billion dollars (mainly in chemicals), transferred to Belgium almost an exact duplicate of its U.S. plant manufacturing hydroxyethelcellulose. Accordingly, the process engineering was completely copied and the detailed engineering involved only modifying the U.S. drawings to conform to the site conditions and metric standards. The transfer proceeded smoothly, although considerable expense in prestartup operator training was incurred.

Case 4

A small U.S. firm with quite limited international operations decided to manufacture abroad hydraulic hose assemblies, couplings and tubing. The equipment from an existing facility was transferred lock, stock and barrel to the new site. There was a minimal engineering expense involved, since copies were simply made of the machine layout drawings of the parent plant.

The technology for manufacturing these products is essentially embodied in the machines. Technology transfer involved transporting the equipment, lining it up and learning how to operate it. Most of the transfer costs arose from the latter activity, as it took several years for labor productivity and materials efficiency to rise to the standards achieved in the parent plant. According to the firm, part of the problem arose from using second-hand machinery. Some of the machines were old, temperamental and quite idiosyncratic. This complicated the learning process considerably. There was no prestart-up training provided, although one skilled operator from the parent facility was transferred to the location abroad to assist in the training of the labor force.

Case 5

A division of a large U.S. electronics multinational transferred to Taiwan technology to assemble and test integrated circuits. This was the second product line to be transferred to this subsidiary. The technology was identical to that used in the U.S.A. Manufacture of the most complicated component—the wafer—was kept in the U.S.A. because of the learning economies associated with wafer manufacture.[1] Because of the shallow learning curves typically experienced with all phases of integrated circuit manufacture, excess manufacturing costs were relatively high. Through-put yields were only 25 percent at the beginning of the startup phase.

Case 6

A large U.S. conglomerate with over a century of experience at manufacturing abroad transferred to its French subsidiary the technology to manufacture a new model of a complex consumer durable.

This particular model represented an advance in the state of the art. The model embodied a fundamental design change and a fundamental change in materials. The new model was thus developed in the United States, first commercialized in France and sold in high income markets throughout the world. Many of the components were sourced from outside France, particularly from Italy and the developing countries.

Case 7

A large multinational firm well known in the chemical industry transferred to a subsidiary in Australia the technology to manufacture polyethelene packaging film. The firm regarded the technology as one of the more complex it possessed. The plant established abroad was quite small and identical to a facility in the U.S. Posttransfer materials efficiency and labor productivity was on a par with the U.S. operation. Total project costs abroad were higher than the U.S. because of higher equipment and shipping costs, travel expense and the training costs for a labor force not familiar with packaging film technology. Accordingly, excess manufacturing costs were higher than they would have been in the U.S. Furthermore, there were prestartup training expenses: an engineer was brought to the U.S. for several months of prestartup training. Furthermore, the U.S. parent sent two people abroad for five weeks—the duration of the manufacturing startup.

Case 8

A U.S. multinational with annual sales under $100 million transferred chlorinated solvents technology to a Swedish firm. The process was unique to the transferor. Although the transferor had never manufactured chlorinated solvents, it had been involved in their application for many years. A licensing package providing technical assistance was arranged and the transfer proceeded smoothly, despite the fact that the transferor had no manufacturing experience in the relevant area.

Case 9

A U.S. multinational with annual sales under $100 million transferred chlorinated solvents technology to a Japanese joint venture. Engineering and design proceeded in Japan, and costs were twice what they would have been in the U.S.A.: most of this was attributed to translation and conversion costs and to the differences in the managerial philosophies of the parties to the transfer. Some adaptations to the design were necessary to take account of different feedstocks. The operating characteristics of the plant fully come up to those of the U.S. facility.

Case 10

A U.S. multinational with annual sales of less than $100 million established a facility to manufacture a vinyl chloride monomer in an Eastern European country. The U.S. multinational had already established several such plants of its own in the U.S. No equity was held by the transferor in the venture. No unexpected technical problems were encountered. The transferor provided extensive consultation (one man for two years, together with liaison support for him in the U.S.).

Case 11

A U.S. multinational transferred to its Dutch subsidiary a new and very different model of a highly complex item of office equipment. The development of this item proceeded in the U.S. The transfer to Holland of this product also represented first commercialization. The project represented the largest capital investment that this midsized multinational had ever made. The decision to conduct first commercialization abroad was influenced by the fact that the foreign subsidiary was already involved in manufacturing this class of product, but sales were declining, and a superior product was needed to revitalize the foreign operation. Hence, the U.S. parent decided to transfer the technology abroad and upgrade the labor force to the extent that was necessary.

The transfer was expensive because of distance, delays, language barriers and disruption to domestic operations. A complete team of engineers was sent abroad to facilitate the transfer.

Case 12

A chemical process was transferred from the European subsidiary to the parent facility of a U.S. multinational. It was a relatively small project (total costs under $1 million), and the transferee performed most of the transfer activities. Technical personnel were sent abroad to assimilate the technology and then perform the necessary design procedures to ensure its successful application in the U.S. facility. Application involved extensive modification to an already existing obsolete plant.[2] Because of some design improvements, transferee operating performance was marginally superior to that of the transferors.

Case 13

A large U.S. engineering contractor took the initiative and secured access to a process to manufacture polybutadiene and transferred this technology under a licensing agreement to an Eastern European organization that already had many years of experience manufacturing this product by a different process. The engineering company performed most of the engineering and provided a great deal of the technical support. The technology was about ten years old, and was transferred with success.

Case 14

A large, diversified U.S. multinational chemical firm transferred to a consortium of Japanese firms process technology to manufacture chlorine and caustic soda by electrolysis of brine. The process had already undergone many applications both in the U.S. and abroad. The transfer was accordingly very straightforward.

Case 15

A U.S. multinational transferred to Argentina the technology required for the operation of a large volume petrochemical project. This was a "greenfields" operation. The engineering was performed by a U.S. firm that had engineered many similar plants abroad, and no special problems were encountered in the transfer.

Case 16

A large U.S. multinational oil company established a petroleum refinery in Canada embodying an improved reforming catalyst. A pilot plant had previously utilized the technology in the U.S. Although engineering costs were high, excess manufacturing costs were relatively low compared to the sample averages. This is typical for refinery startups. The transfer was regarded as very routine since most of the firm's refining capacity is located outside of the U.S.A.

Case 17

The U.S. subsidiary of a European multinational transferred to a sister subsidiary in Europe the technology to manufacture an aerospace engine bearing. The bearing used vacuum-melted steels and was considered a major innovation in aerospace bearings: it was of superior quality and had a life much longer than conventional bearings. The technology was transferred under license: the U.S. subsidiary provided all relevant applied research information, product design information and process development information. The transfer proceeded smoothly, but only because the transferor and transferee had been in the roller bearing business for many years. Accordingly, transfer costs were low, and infinitesimal compared to the initial R & D costs associated with producing the technology.

Case 18

A U.S. multinational established a joint venture to manufacture carpet yarns in Brazil. The technology was familiar to the transferor as it had already been applied in the U.S.A. Because of exchange controls in the host country most of the civil and detailed engineering was performed by Brazilian firms. Because of the extra supervision required, this increased the transfer costs over what they might otherwise have been. The transfer nevertheless proceeded smoothly, and startups were lower than they would have been in the U.S., since labor productivity was up to par with the U.S., but wage rates were considerably below U.S. levels.

Case 19

This is an atypical case in which a U.S. multinational transferred acrylics technology to its Mexican subsidiary from an independent German firm with its plant located in Germany. The U.S. parent did not have in-house the technology that its Mexican subsidiary desired, so it chose instead to search elsewhere for an appropriate process. An arrangement was made to license a German process that was operating in the plant where it had evolved over a number of years. The process was translated into blueprints, but because the plant had undergone a myriad of changes, it was extremely difficult to identify the key elements of the design. Accordingly, the process had to be "invented" in many respects as the transfer proceeded. Although a four to six week manufacturing startup was projected, the startup actually took 18 months. As a result, transfer costs were quite high.

Case 20

A large Japanese multinational firm secured from a U.S. firm the technical specifications of a high speed line printer. Despite the fact that the Japanese firm had no previous manufacturing experience in this product line (it was previously engaged in electromechanical instrumentation), there was no significant interaction between the transferor and transferee. Documentation and a sample product were secured from the transferor, and that was essentially the extent of the interaction. Practically all of the transfer costs were incurred by the transferee, yet these were remarkably low, and a source of surprise to the transferor.

Case 21

A large multinational U.S.-based oil company transferred to one of its European subsidiaries an entirely new process to manufacture a specialty oil. The technology was perceived by the transferor as being quite complex. It involved a new class of catalysts and required a degree of manufacturing sophistication not previously demanded of the transferee. Nevertheless, the transfer was regarded as a complete success.

Case 22

This project was small scale and involved the transfer of assembly technology associated with the production of signal generators. The transfer proceeded in a stepwise fashion: the assemblies sent were gradually disaggregated until only the most elemental units were sent. That is, subassemblies were transferred first, and when these could be assembled proficiently, individual components were sent. Usable output did emerge during the startup, but productivity was initially only 40 percent of target.

Case 23

A large U.S. multinational chemical company licensed aluminum flouride technology to a company in North Africa. The engineering was performed by a French contractor. The facilities were quite standard, except for adaptations that were necessary to meet the special requirements of the desert environment. The transferee had no previous manufacturing experience, so the operators and managers recruited received considerable prestartup training in the U.S. The transfer was a success.

Case 24

A large U.S. multinational chemical firm licensed sulfur hexaflouride technology to a Japanese chemicals and glass manufacturer. The plant was a scaled down replica of a U.S. facility. Although the plant was relatively small, it was nevertheless highly sophisticated. If the technology is not implemented precisely according to specifications, transfer can be a complete disaster. The transferee had over 50 years of manufacturing experience. The Japanese contractor was highly efficient in engineering and construction, the result being that total project costs were considerably lower than they would have been in the U.S.

Case 25

A U.S. multinational firm with annual sales of about one-half billion dollars transferred to its U.K. subsidiary a new process to manufacture methylmethacryliate (this is used in the production of plexiglass). Although this process had already been applied in a commercial size plant in the U.S., the U.K. plant represented a tremendous scale-up of the operation. In retrospect, the U.S. plant, although of commercial size, could properly be regarded as a pilot plant since the parent firm was continually learning about the process from its operations in the U.S. plant, and much of the new knowledge was incorporated into the design of the U.K. facility. The U.K. subsidiary was hitherto quite small and had no R & D facilities. Its involvement in the transfer activities was minimal. Besides the scale factor, there were few adaptations to the plant besides modifications to the cooling system made possible by the lower temperatures prevailing at the British locations.

Case 26

A U.S. multinational with annual sales of about one-half billion dollars transferred to its U.K. subsidiary a completely new process to manufacture acrylites. The company regarded the process as one of the most sophisticated it had developed and applied. Although the "front end" of the process was a scale-up of an older technology, the "back end" was entirely new. The process represented a considerable technical advance and produced a purer product with lower undesired by-product.

Process development and project design proceeded simultaneously for almost two and one half years. Accordingly, and although the process was to be first commercialized in the U.K., engineering for the process and project was conducted in the firm's own engineering facilities in the U.S.A. It would have been prohibitively expensive to attempt parallel activity of development and engineering design in the U.S. and the U.K. respectively. First commercialization of this new process proceeded in the U.K. because of marketing considerations. Extra capacity was needed in Europe, and so it made sense to commercialize abroad, despite the considerable technical difficulties and extra expense that the company encountered.

Case 27

A division of a large U.S. multinational transferred a family of protective relays to its Puerto Rican subsidiary. The subsidiary had been established a decade earlier and the U.S. parent felt that with ten years of accumulated experience, this subsidiary could absorb any type of assembly technology that the parent cared to send over. This particular transfer was complicated, however, because the technology was quite old and was poorly documented. Nevertheless, posttransfer productivity and quality were higher than in the U.S. parent.

Case 28

A U.S. firm with a century of operating experience abroad transferred to its Dutch subsidiary the technology to manufacture an electromechanical device that has a computational function. The plant was involved essentially in assembly rather than parts fabrication. The U.S. plant was removed and reassembled in the subsidiary. Minimal engineering and startup assistance was provided by the transferor. Because the technology for electromechanical devices is changing very rapidly, R & D personnel were involved in the transfer, but this is not generally necessary for the transfer of most products that this firm manufactures.

Case 29

A U.S. oil company entered a joint venture with a chemical company to establish a large refinery on the Asian mainland. The basic engineering was performed by an American contractor. The detailed engineering and procurement was performed by an indigenous contractor. Prestartup training was provided for 150 people. Startup costs were remarkably low.

NOTES

1. For a discussion of this consideration, see W. Finan, "International Transfer of Semiconductor Technology Through U.S.-Based Firms" (M.B.A. thesis, University of Pennsylvania, 1974).

2. Adjustments were made to the capital cost data to ensure that capital costs were measured on the same basis as they were for the other projects.

Appendix B:
Definitions of Variables

Most of the variables in the study have rather precise definitions, and unless the definition is unambiguously clear, it is stated below.

FIRM CHARACTERISTICS

Sales
This is defined as the U.S. dollar value of total sales originating in the "home"[1] territory, i.e., the dollar value of domestic production used to satisfy "domestic" or export demand.

Manufacturing Experience
This is defined as the length of time manufacturing operations have been conducted in a given four digit ISIC[2] industry up to the time of the commencement of the startup phase of the transfer project.

Research and Development/Sales
Defined as total "home" research and development expenditures of the firm divided by total sales, as defined above.

TECHNOLOGY CHARACTERISTICS

Age
This is defined as the number of years between first commercial implementation of the technology anywhere in the world, and the

end of the technology transfer program.[3] (The beginning of first commercial implementation will be different from the end of the development phase by the extent to which there is overlap with the manufacturing startup phase.)

Number of Previous Manufacturing Startups

This is defined as the number of times previous to this transfer that the most critical innovation underlying this technology has been incorporated in a manufacturing startup.

Number of Firms

"Number of firms" is the total number of other firms that have utilized this innovation, or a competitive variation of it.

Time Taken for Transfer

This is defined as the number of months between the time when both parties reach formal agreement to proceed with the transfer and the time the startup of the plant was formally terminated.

Materials Efficiency

This is the ratio of usuable final product to total final product.

NOTES

1. "Home" territory is defined as the operating domain of the firm. Thus, if the transferor is the parent of a multinational enterprise, then the sales value of the subsidiary are not included in total sales of the transferor.

2. See United Nations, *International Standard Industrial Classification of all Economic Activities*, United Nations Statistical Papers, Series M, no. 4 (New York, 1968).

3. If there is more than one key innovation embodied in the technology, then the date of commercial implementation of the most recent key innovation is the reference date. Age is defined as the time to the end of the transfer program, since any knowledge about the technology acquired up to this point is potentially useful for the transfer. For first commercialization, age will be the transfer time minus the development overlap (if any).

Bibliography

Bibliography

Arrow, K. .K. Classificatory notes on the production and transmission of technological knowledge. *American Economic Review: Papers and Proceedings* 52:29-35 (May 1969).

_____. Comment. In Universities—National Bureau Committee for Economic Research, *The Rate and Direction of Inventive Activity.* Princeton: Princeton University Press, 1962.

_____. The organization of economic activity. In *The Analysis and Evaluation of Public Expenditures: The PPB System*, 1. Joint Economic Committee, 91st Cong., Washington, D.C., 1969.

Arditti, F. On the separation of production from the developer. *Journal of Business* 41:317-28 (July 1968).

Bain, J. *Industrial Organization.* New York: John Wiley, 1968.

Baldwin, R.E. International trade in inputs and outputs. *American Economic Review; Papers and Proceedings* 60:430-34 (May 1970).

Baranson, J. *Manufacturing Problems in India: The Cummins Diesel Experience.* Syracuse, N.Y.: Syracuse University Press, 1967.

_____. Technical improvement in developing countries. *Finance and Development* 11:2-5 (June 1974).

_____. Technology transfer through the international firm. *American Economic Review; Papers and Proceedings* 60:435-40 (May 1970).

Bar-Zakay, S. Technology transfer model. *Industrial Research and Development News* 6:1-11 (1972).

Berrill, K., ed. *Economic Development with Special Reference to East Asia.* New York: St. Martins Press, 1964.

Carter, G. Directed licensing: an evaluation of a proposed technique for reducing the procurement cost of aircraft. Santa Monica, Cal.: The Rand Corporation, R-1604-PR.

Caves, R.E. International corporations: the industrial economics of foreign investment. *Economica* 38:1-27 (February 1971).

Chow, G.C. Tests of equality between sets of coefficients in two linear regressions. *Econometrica* 28:591-605 (July 1960).

Finan, W. International transfer of semiconductor technology through U.S.-based firms. M.B.A. Thesis, University of Pennsylvania, 1974.

Freeman, C. Discussion of the paper by Professor Trickovic. In B.R. Williams, ed., *Science and Technology in Economic Growth.* New York: John Wiley, 1973.

_____. Research and development in electronic capital goods. *National Institute Economic Review* 34:1-70 (November 1965).

Gallagher, J. Efficient estimation of worldwide plants cost. *Chemical Engineering* June 2, 1962, pp. 196-202.

Gillette, R. Latin America: is imported technology too expensive? *Science* 181:4-44 (July 1973).

Gruber, W., and Marquis, D., eds. *Factors in the Transfer of Technology* (Cambridge, M.I.T. Press, 1969).

Hall, G.R., and Johnson, R.E. Transfers of United States aerospace technology to Japan. In R. Vernon, ed., *The Technology Factor in International Trade.* New York: National Bureau of Economic Research, 1970.

Hayami, Y., and Ruttan, V. *Agricultural Development and International Perspective.* Baltimore: Johns Hopkins, 1971.

Henderson, W.O. *Britain and Industrial Europe: 1750-1870.* Leicester, England: Leicester University Press, 1972.

International Bank for Reconstruction and Development. *World Bank Atlas.* Washington, D.C., 1973.

Japanese Ministry of International Trade and Industry. *Gijutsu Dohkoh Chosa Hohkokusho* (Report on the Trend of Technology). Tokyo, 1963.

Johnson, R. Costs of overseas plants. *Chemical Engineering* 76:146-52 (March 10, 1969).

Johnson, H.G. The efficiency and welfare implications of the international corporation. In C.P. Kindleberger, ed., *The International Corporation.* Cambridge, Mass.: M.I.T. Press, 1970.

Jones, D. The 'extra costs' in Europe's biggest synthetic fiber complex at Mogilev, U.S.S.R. *Worldwide Projects and Installations* 7:30-35 (May-June 1973).

Kreinin, M.E. Comparative labor effectiveness and the Leontief scarce-factor paradox. *American Economic Review* 55:131-40 (March 1965).

Kuznets, Simon. *Modern Economic Growth: Rate Structure, and Spread.* New Haven: Yale University Press, 1966.

Leontief, W. On assignment of patent rights on inventions made under government research contracts. *Harvard Law Review* 7:492-97 (January 1964).

Lewis, W.A. Economic development with unlimited supplies of labor. *The Manchester School* 22:139-91 (May 1954).

Mansfield, E. Discussion of the paper by Professor Griliches. In B.R. Williams, ed., *Science and Technology in Economic Growth.* New York: John Wiley, 1973.

Mansfield, E.; Rapoport, J.; Schnee, J.; Wagner, S.; and Hamburger, M. *Research and Innovation in the Modern Corporation.* New York: W.W. Norton, 1971.

Mason, R. Hal. The multinational firm and the cost of technology to developing countries. *California Management Review* 15:5-13 (Summer 1973).

Meursinge, J. Practical experience in the transfer of technology. *Technology and Culture* 12:469-70 (July 1971).

McGraw-Hill Encycloped of Science and Technology. New York: McGraw-Hill, 1960. Vols. 4, 10.

National Academy of Sciences. *U.S. International Firms and R, D, and E in Developing Countries.* Washington, D.C., 1973.

Oshima, K. Research and development and economic growth in Japan. In B.R. Williams, ed., *Science and Technology in Economic Growth.* New York: John Wiley, 1973.

Perlmutter, H.V. Social architectural problems of the multinational firm. *Quarterly Journal of AIESEC International* 3 (August 1967).

Reynolds, L. Discussion. *American Economic Review* 56:112-14 (May 1966).

Robinson, E.A.G. Discussion of the paper by Professor Hsia. In B.R. Williams, ed., *Science and Technology in Economic Growth.* New York: John Wiley, 1973.

Rodriguez, C.A. Trade in technical knowledge and the national advantage. *Journal of Political Economy* 83:121-35 (February 1975).

Rosenberg, N. Economic development and the transfer of technology: some historical perspectives. *Technology and Culture* 11:550-75 (October 1970).

Scaperlanda, A.E., and Mauser, L.J. The determinants of U.S. direct investment in the E.E.C. *American Economic Review* 59:558-68 (September 1969).

Scherer, F.M. Government research and development programs. In R. Dorfman, ed., *Measuring the Benefits of Government Expenditures.* Washington, D.C.: The Brookings Institution, 1965.

Schumacher, E.F. The work of the intermediate technology development group in Africa. *International Labor Review* 106:75-92 (July 1972).

Spencer, D.L. *Technology Gap in Perspective.* New York: Spartan Books, 1970.

Tilton, J.E. *International Diffusion of Technology: The Case of Semiconductors.* Washington, D.C.: The Brookings Institute, 1971).

United Nations. *International Standard Industrial Classification of all Economic Activities.* United Nations Statistical Papers, series M, No. 4. New York, 1968.

United Nations Conference on Trade and Development. The transfer of technology. *Journal of World Trade Law* 4:692-718 (September-October 1970).

Vernon, R. International investment and international trade in the product cycle. *Quarterly Journal of Economics* 80:190-207 (May 1966).

Williamson, O.E. *Markets and Hierarchies: Analysis and Antitrust Implications.* New York: Free Press, 1975.

Yen, Yen-Chen. Estimating plant costs in the developing countries. *Chemical Engineering* 79:89-92 (July 10, 1972).

Index

About the Author

David J. Teece is Assistant Professor of Business Economics at the Graduate School of Business, Stanford
University. He received a Bachelors and Masters degree
(with first class honors) from the University of Canterbury, and an
M.A. and Ph.D. in Economics from the University of Pennsylvania.
His main research interests are in industrial organization and the
economics of technological change, focusing in particular on international issues. He is the author of *Vertical Integration and Vertical
Divestiture in the U.S. Oil Industry* (Stanford University Institute for
Energy Studies, 1976), and "Time-Cost Tradeoffs: Elasticity Estimates and Determinants for International Technology Transfer Projects," forthcoming in *Management Science*. Professor Teece is cur-
rently studying overseas R&D by U.S. multinationals, and research
and innovation in the U.S. oil industry.